CW00683804

Police to Paranoia

Police to Paranoia

My true story of when I was sectioned
under the Mental Health Act as a
serving police officer

REBECCA J HOUSE

Copyright © 2023 by Rebecca J House

All rights reserved. No part of this book may be reproduced or used in any manner without written permission of the copyright owner except for the use of quotations in a book review.

ISBNs
Paperback: 978-1-80541-119-2
eBook: 978-1-80541-118-5

INTRODUCTION

I woke up at 9am. The first thing I wanted to do was go outside in the fresh air for a walk. I wasn't locked in my room, but I wasn't allowed outside either. The room was small and plain, with white walls, approximately four feet by six feet, probably not dissimilar to a prison cell. To my right there was a wardrobe with no hangers, just shelves, and a small grey chair – it was heavy so you couldn't throw it, and even if I found the strength, I still couldn't as it was fastened to the floor. Infront of me was a small white sink, that small it looked like it belonged in a dolls house. To my left there was a large window with thin metal bars running vertically down the pane only letting bits of the sun outside shine through, teasing me that there was life out there but I couldn't be part of it as I was locked in here. What was I doing here? I wanted to leave immediately. There's nothing wrong with me I thought. Eventually realisation hit and I knew I was wrong. The reality was I was in a very bad way, I had lost my mind.

Now in my forties, and fifteen years ago whilst I was a serving police officer, I was sectioned under the

Mental Health Act on a 136 having suffered a psychotic breakdown. If you're mentally unwell and are deemed to be unable to consent to treatment, this legislation sets out when people can be detained and treated in hospital against their will. This book is a true story about how I got there, and my experience whilst being detained on a psychiatric facility, what it was like whilst I was there and how I survived it and got better. Not forgetting the vital lesson, I learnt, that mental health can affect absolutely anyone despite their gender, age and profession.

Whilst reading this book you may ask: "Yes, but did this actually happen? Are you sure you remember correctly? "Yes, but what did you do to provoke this?" "Yes, but were you not a threat to other people?" Yes, but you were sick, you deserved this treatment."

The thing you have to remember about a person experiencing psychosis is that they do not interpret their surroundings in a normal way: during my mental health crisis episode, all things and people around me became metaphors. Police officers, paramedics or hospital security guards were not just people to me, they represented force, harm and danger, and being a police officer myself this made it even scarier and more confusing.

When it comes to violence by authority figures, public conversation in this moment in time is revolving. But in my mind, speaking from my experiences, this is just the tip of the iceberg. We have seen video footage of the surface of Mars and the Titanic at the bottom of the ocean but the general public is totally unaware of what goes on inside the locked doors of psych wards. News cameras are not allowed on these floors, and patients are not allowed to record on their phones. In fact, I wasn't even allowed a phone in there fifteen years ago. As a result, the general public do not see how much violence is perpetrated against psych ward patients.

In my day-to-day experience, I haven't met any people talking about violence against the mentally ill, because most people experiencing psychosis-related violence are not in a position to speak up. Many of them are mentally unable to advocate for themselves, and many live with too much shame to share their story as I did until now. After all, who wants to broadcast to the world that their mental illness was so bad that you had to be removed from your own home by the cops, being a cop yourself? Who wants to broadcast to the world that they spent time in a psych ward?

Instead, if we are lucky enough to have caring family around us as I was, we hide out in their spare bedroom, stewing in our shame, carrying not only the trauma of our illness but then also the trauma inflicted on us by those entrusted with our care and recovery during our hospitalisation.

CHAPTER ONE

As a child I always had lots of friends and had a privileged and happy upbringing. 'Life was fun, simple'. I was always at my happiest when I was with my family, my mum, dad and sister. Family holidays were the best and I had no issues or worries throughout my earlier years. As a teenager I continued to love life and enjoyed the transition to high school where I was part of a popular group of girls. Like all teenagers I studied and socialised throughout and continued with this through college and university. My love for the police determined my path for study choices where I went on to do a degree in psychology and criminology.

From the young age of five I always knew what I wanted to do when I grew up. There was no doubt in my mind that I would be a police officer one day. I guess applying to go to an undertakers for work experience at the age of sixteen made me realise I had a morbid fascination for things early on. So that is what I went on to become and at the age of twenty-one I applied for the role of a police officer and after weeks of research and hard graft I submitted my application. Whilst waiting to hear I packed my bag and went off travelling round Canada for three months. It was whilst I was there that I found out I had passed the first stage of the recruitment process and when I returned from my travels, I went on to pass the further assessments. Before I knew it, I was at my passing out parade being sworn in to be a police officer. I had to pinch myself at times as I couldn't believe I had succeeded in a job that I had wanted to do since the age of five. Me an officer of the law, WOW! I've always strived to live a good life and wanted to help people less fortunate than myself so being a police officer has always made this so real for me.

At the age of twenty-two I went off to training school to start my life in the force and the next six months were full of laughter, ups and downs and hard work both physically and mentally but definitely the best six months yet. I finished my training and got my first posting to Blackpool which was an eyeopener but the best experience I could have been given. They say if you're posted there you 'sink' or 'swim' and I'm proud to say I swam my little arms off and kept my head above water in what was the most challenging and difficult two years of my life so far. I survived it though and went on to work on the Public Protection Unit dealing with those on the Sex Offenders Register. I thought being in uniform was a rewarding job, however working on this unit took rewarding to a new level. Being able to protect young children and vulnerable people was the best job I could ask for.

Chapter One

It was during my early years in the police that I finally admitted to myself that I was gay. I had had feelings for a very long time and like many other people tried to block them out. I used to tell myself, I'm not gay, but what if I am? What will my family and friends say? I don't want this life, I want a family – kids. It wasn't until I met my first long term partner that I really admitted it to myself and eventually to my family and friends as I was finally content with how I felt and who I wanted to be. I had accepted it and was now ready for those close to me to accept it too. All my friends and family were incredible about it and for the first time in a long time I felt complete. A new partner, who I was now living with, my dream job, family and friends who supported me. Things couldn't be better until I got the call in the middle of the night to tell me my Nanna had died. The phone call that changed my life in ways that I would never have thought and the next six months to come were not only filled with grief but fear, and changes in my content life that are beyond anything that I could ever have imagined. Getting that kind of call late at night was very hard to take in as I had literally spoken to her a few hours earlier. It was as though my dad was speaking in slow motion and not making any sense, but in fact it was my brain trying to process it all or not process it so I didn't have to make it reality.

CHAPTER TWO

I was very close to my Nanna, for a number of reasons, and her passing so suddenly and being the first significant death, I had personally experienced, affected me massively. I have seen lots of trauma and death as a police officer, but dealing with the death and loss of a loved one, a family member is obviously completely different. My Nanna had many qualities and taught me many valuable lessons in life. She was strong, kind, generous and courageous. She was a very strong woman who could adapt herself to any new challenging situation. Maybe she derived that strength from growing up in Berlin during the war and witnessing horrific incidents. Maybe I was to later learn that strength from her and never realised it at the time.

I carried on at work and my daily life as best I could whilst dealing with the grief and loss but I just didn't feel myself. It was as though a piece of me had died with my Nanna and I started to become withdrawn and vacant from everyone and everything. It wasn't long after her death that my long-term relationship broke down which was solely down to me and something I am not proud of. I developed feelings for someone who I genuinely cared a lot about but in the process ruined the one good thing in my life at that time. I've never been good at dealing with guilt and hurting others and to this day I shall always regret my actions and how I went about things but I can't change that now and can only learn from past experiences and believe you me, that I have. Within a space of six months my whole world had been turned upside down. I tried to fix the relationship and I really wanted to make it work but I couldn't. Not because I didn't want to but because I no longer felt like me anymore. My bubbly, outgoing personality was slipping away. Looking back on it now, I believe I was grieving two major losses in my life, my Nanna and my long-term partner. Alongside this I was also overwhelmed with the guilt from hurting two people I deeply cared for, that being my partner and the other person I had developed feelings for. I've always been a sensitive person, more so than others and the guilt was too much to bear.

I carried on going into work but my concentration got poorer by the day and before I knew it my job was totally affected. I had lost my motivation, no longer put the extra hours in which I regularly did and my paperwork became sloppy. My friends and colleagues grew concerned as I hardly spoke anymore and my work which I was always so proud of was not the same. I was always the last to leave in my office as I wanted to make sure I had done everything right. However, now, I couldn't wait to get out of the door and clock watched every single second till home time. Over the weeks it just got worse and worse and I couldn't understand what was happening. I was a police officer, I was a professional, I was happy go lucky Beck. What was happening to me? I kept saying to myself snap out of it, you've messed up, you've lost your Nanna but pull yourself together now, however I couldn't. These things happen to millions of people on a daily basis and they get on with it, so why am I so different. Why was my life falling apart in front of me. I started to slip into a dark hole and was falling deeper and deeper every day.

There was one day that was a very bad day for so many reasons, too many to mention but my anxiety was through the roof. I decided to bite the bullet and pick up the phone and make an appointment with the doctor with an attempt to see if they could help me make sense of what was happening to me. I really needed to speak to someone who understood what I was going through and could give me the answers and hopefully fix me. However, as expected, and the reason I had put off going for so long, after a ten-minute appointment of yes and no questions I left with a prescription for anti-depressants. The word depressant depressed me in itself. I'm not a sad person, I don't need these tablets to make me feel 'normal' again. The packet remained on the kitchen unit for the next few days, staring at me, begging me to take them. Finally, after refusing to take them, I gave in and started my course thinking what's the worst that can happen. I think the main reason I did it was to try and reduce the worry for my family and friends and to be seen to be helping myself, however I was still very cynical about it all.

Days passed and I still felt no different. I was desperate and impatient, I hoped the magic pill would kick in and I would start to feel some benefit almost instantly, not that it had to get in my system and may take weeks to take effect.

By this stage I was starting to give up a bit. I had gone off work sick and basically locked myself away at home where I was still living with my ex- partner who had now basically turned into my care giver. As the weeks went on the medication started to take effect but not in a good way. It had started to affect my ability to process information and cope with any situation no matter how small. Taking a shower and eating a meal was done more for survival than pleasure and before I knew it, I didn't know what day of the week it was. Every day was a constant battle, every conversation a struggle and I was no longer functioning rationally. I couldn't believe my role as a police officer with the Public Protection Unit, a position I had worked so hard to secure had slipped away from me. I hadn't been removed from the unit but I knew I couldn't stay on there the way I was. Despite my love for the job, it was impossible for me to go back to work when I couldn't even hold a conversation with my family and friends. What chance did I have of protecting vulnerable people when I couldn't even protect myself. Having always been a strong and resilient person I did not believe that mental health could ever be an issue in my life. The lack of understanding about what was happening to me made my situation more frustrating and scarier and I found myself in a downward spiral.

The days turned into weeks, the weeks into months and I waited patiently for these happy pills to make me happy or at least give me some sense of normality again. However, that day didn't come and before I knew it, I was back at the doctors and given yet again a different set of anti- depressants. I was advised to wean myself off the current ones and then start my new course. I didn't think for one minute that this was the answer but I went with it hoping for some kind of miracle. Every day I woke up I prayed that the new tablets would be working and I could think straight again or at least see some joy or hope at the slightest thing. That day didn't come though and my mental health declined even more. I was hardly eating at this point and along with having to deal with all the other feelings I was going through, these new 'magic pills' decided to throw suicidal thoughts into the mix. They were the kind of thoughts that no one wants to be having, so scary, real and unlike myself that I didn't know how to cope. This started a spiral of depression, panic attacks and low confidence. I spent my time wrapped up in these thoughts, convincing myself that I was a terrible person and losing the confidence to talk to others even more. I didn't recognise myself anymore. You read the side effects of medications but always think it won't happen to me. How wrong I was, as the next few weeks went to a completely different level and my behaviour not only petrified my family but also myself.

I remember waking up one morning and wondering where the nearest tree was that I could tie my dressing gown cord round and my neck to the other end. How could this be happening? I've dealt with jobs like this as a police officer and cut people down and seen the devastating effects it has on people, on families. I didn't want to die or hurt myself, far from it, but I couldn't control the thoughts that were flooding my mind constantly or stop this gut- wrenching feeling in my stomach which I can only describe as constant worry and anxiety. I couldn't imagine not being around anymore but I couldn't see any other way of making this nightmare, this living hell stop. I was basically trapped inside my own brain, being pulled from every angle of despair and desperation. I just wanted the pain to stop. Before I knew it, I was having these thoughts on a daily basis and it wasn't long before I was acting on them. My ex- partner would come home from work to find me hiding in a cupboard with a cord round my neck and me pulling it tight. I was aware of what I was doing but not aware if that makes sense. Again, I didn't want to die, I just wanted this suffocating feeling to go away and to have my life back. I feel like I need to go into more detail about this and try and explain more about how I was feeling, but in all honesty, I can't. I couldn't make sense of it then, and I still can't to this day. If I had to sum it up, I would say it was like someone had jumped inside my body, my brain, and completely taken over it, like the exorcist on TV.

CHAPTER THREE

My brain had completely crashed and I had lost control of everything I was doing. It got so out of control that I attended hospital that day, as I was genuinely concerned for my own life and as the thoughts were so over whelming, I genuinely thought I would act on them, and that would be it. This is one of the scariest things I had to go through, the torment and torture of these feelings was just too much to bear. After hours of waiting in A&E to see the crisis team I was later discharged back home in the care of my ex- partner. Other than discussing my current thoughts and if I felt suicidal at that moment in time, which I didn't, they were happy to let me go. Although I was relieved that I wasn't kept in I was still concerned and scared what my future held. I hadn't so much lied to them when they went through their check list but I suppose I hadn't been completely truthful either and had played things down. There was no offer of counselling or any therapy or any 'label' to my behaviour, however surprise surprise, I was prescribed another set of medication to add to the cocktail of drugs that I was already on. At that time, I was reluctant to take them but thought I could trust the health system and I guess I had to trust that they knew what they were doing. I continued on these for the next few weeks just about managing to get through each day, no specific diagnosis other than 'Depression'. I was starting to think that this was reality as it wasn't the first time it had been mentioned. I knew something major was going on but I knew it was more than this. I knew people who had been depressed and were on happy pills but they didn't have crazy thoughts like me or act like they were losing their mind. Other people weren't convinced they were dying like I was.

I carried on taking the pills still with the belief and hope that one day I would wake up and feel human again. I waited and waited and still that day never came. I was still slipping deeper and deeper into that big black hole. I cut off all communication with my friends who had been so amazing and supportive so far but I just didn't want anyone to see me in this state and to be honest I didn't even have the energy to make conversation no matter how small. I stopped exercising which was always a passion of mine, especially running. No matter how stressed I was or was having an off day, I always felt better after a run. However, that no longer worked and I didn't have the energy to walk, let alone run. Despite this I lost so much weight through both the stress and adrenaline of everything going on. The suicidal thoughts started to get stronger and I continued to act things out in my head and then sneak out late at night trying to find places to be alone and potentially act my thoughts out. I always contacted someone though so this in itself shows that I never wanted to hurt myself, or succeed at ending my life. It was desperation, panic, confusion. I also started to scratch my wrists with a knife. It would be too much to say I was self-harming as I never cut myself and have no scars to show but I guess I was close to this and testing myself as to how far I would go. It was a distraction, even if it was only for a few minutes.

My doctor was made aware of this latest development and I was prescribed diazepam. I'd obviously heard of this drug but Wow, I had no idea how effective it was. If I was having a particularly bad day or wanted to build up the confidence to leave my home then I would pop one of these tiny pills in my mouth and hey presto I felt normal. It was an instant hit of a combination of relief, relaxation and most importantly normality. They actually made me feel like I was back to ME. I was able to hold a normal conversation, see joy in life again and actually be positive about the future. However, this didn't last long, an hour maybe, two at most, then it hit me like a sledgehammer in the face. As the pill started to wear off so did my positive attitude and before I knew it, I was back to my paranoid miserable self, trapped in my own body screaming inside to feel that fix again. Yes, it was good to have a couple of hours of relief, but going back to that living hell was probably worse. Feeling happy again and then losing it so suddenly was torture. When I was getting that high, I often thought if I could be prescribed these on a permanent basis and just basically live the rest my life on tablets. Despite being in cuckoo land even I knew this wasn't a realistic plan so took what I was given and never asked for them again as I didn't want the pain of going ten steps forward, ten steps back.

During all this my sister, who I had always been extremely close to was living in America. She was so concerned about me that she flew home for the weekend and my mum treated us to a spa weekend in the Lake District. This is my ideal weekend as I love a good pamper, what girl doesn't. However, whilst there I just couldn't find the fun or enjoyment in any of it despite how hard I tried. All I could think about was dying and wasn't shy to express my thoughts to my sister who seemed completely shocked and bewildered by my behaviour. We hadn't spent any time alone since I had got ill so she was only used to her laid back, happy go lucky sister. Not the sister that had become so withdrawn and convinced she was dying. I probably under estimated at the time how difficult this probably was to see me like this. Not only did I have suicidal thoughts but now the idea that I was actually dying. Of what, I wasn't sure, but over the next coming weeks this thought just got stronger and stronger.

CHAPTER FOUR

When I was discharged from A&E weeks earlier the crisis team said they would keep in touch. I guess you can say the odd phone call was 'keeping in touch' but as far as helping me, that they did not do. I knew I'd got to the stage where there was no magic wand but all I wanted was someone to help me and to help me make sense of all this madness. My family grew increasingly concerned as they could see their daughter slipping away. They didn't know the ins and outs of everything as I wanted to protect them as best as possible but what they could see and knew was already too much for them to bear. My mum grew that concerned that she came and stayed with me for a few days. It was during this time that things went beyond repair and the unimaginable happened one Monday morning that changed my life forever.

That Monday morning, I woke up and strangely felt a little better, not sure if that was the comfort of having my mum there next to me, or that the new medication had completely numbed me. Thinking about it, it was probably a combination of the two. I got up as normal dreading the day ahead, trying to put a bit of a front on for my mum so she didn't know exactly how much of her daughter she had lost. The crisis team came for their first visit to the house to check on me and see how things were going. They couldn't have picked a worse day. Looking back on it I have tried to figure out why things went so wrong that day and in particular the day they happened to come. In all honestly, I still haven't figured out the answer but the only thing I can think, is the thought of other people, people who didn't know me, were stood in my home, my safe place questioning whether I was safe to remain there. We were sat in the lounge talking, what about I can't remember, when all of a sudden something just switched off in my brain. It was as though someone had come behind me and hit me over the head with a sledge hammer knocking me unconscious. However, I wasn't unconscious, but I wasn't conscious either, probably somewhere in the middle. I can't remember things clearly after this but what I do remember is still terrifying to this day. I was rolling around on the floor shouting "I'm dying, help me". I had no idea what was happening but the flash backs of the next half hour still send chills down my body. I remember my mum trying to calm me down which wasn't working in the slightest as I was in a complete trance and had zoned out from everything and everyone around me. I do however remember my ex- partner on the phone asking for the police. The police? But I'm the police. She was the police? Why was she calling them? I wasn't being violent or making threats in any way but at the same time I'd completely gone somewhere in my mind, and there was no coming back.

I could see the crisis team out of the corner of my eye just stood there on their phones. It was like I was having an out of body experience and this wasn't me rolling around on the floor like a scared vulnerable child. I genuinely thought I was dying and although I had been poorly for a while now this was the moment that my psychosis completely kicked in and took over my entire brain and body. I had gone from nought to sixty in literally seconds. Despite the madness, and mayhem that was going on, mainly from me but also the shouts from my mum and ex- partner to calm down, I can still recall the knock on the door and what was to be my fate awaiting me on the other side. Three uniformed police officers then entered our home, my 'safe' place. I could hear muttering going on between the crisis team and the officers, the next minute they walked towards me in silence and started to apply handcuffs to my wrists. No attempt at any communication or trying to calm me down and give me a chance, just straight in with the cuffs. It was absolutely horrendous to be in that situation and handcuffed by my own colleagues and to be restrained when all I needed was help. This was the first of many restraints to come. Obviously, I wasn't going with them without a struggle and started to lash out, not in an attempt to hurt anyone but to resist and stop them from taking me away to a place that soon became hell and indescribable to anyone that has never been taken there before.

The officers finally got the handcuffs on my wrists tightening them that much that they cut my left wrist, where I have the scar as proof to this day. I've been contemplating recently whether to have this scar covered over as it's a constant reminder of that day. However, I've come to the conclusion that it should be left as it is as it shouldn't be seen as a negative but a positive of how strong I am and how I survived such a dreadful traumatic time. They picked me up by my feet and arms and carted me out of my home, past the crisis team, my ex- partner and most importantly my poor mum who looked broken. I will never forget that look of desperation, hurt and trauma in her eyes. My poor mum.

They carried me out along the hall, still dressed in my pjs and outside to where the van was waiting. I could hear the back doors bang open and they basically threw me inside it onto the floor with no respect for me as a human being, let alone one of them, a police officer. The last thing I could hear was the laughter of the officers and one of them saying "Who's having this one?" as in who wants the arrest as theirs. This comment has always stayed with me as I thought they would have had a bit of compassion for what they were witnessing. As police officers, you are taught to treat mental health patients with the respect they deserve and me being that patient and also an officer

I would have expected slightly different behaviour. It's not that I wanted to be treated differently because of my profession, just treated with a bit of dignity I suppose.

The journey to the police station seemed to take forever and the only sound I could hear was that of my heart pounding faster and faster as though I was near the end of a marathon. I was still lying on the cold metal floor of the van with my hands to the back of me and my feet wedged to the opposite side in attempt to stop myself banging into the sides as the van went steadily along the roads hitting the occasional pot hole. The van still smelt of the last person that had had the pleasure of being in here, a combination of the sweet smell of sweat and stale booze. How the hell had I got to this. My mind was everywhere at this point but despite having dealt with jobs like this as an officer I still couldn't comprehend that I had been arrested or detained under the Mental Health Act. Whatever you want to call it I had had my dignity stripped in the last half hour and had never felt so scared in my entire life.

The van came to a sudden stop and I heard the driver's door open and mumbling between two people. The back door flung open and the brightness of the sunshine hit my eyes as it had been so dark and dingy in the cage that I had been placed in for the last ten minutes. The two officers climbed in and grabbed an arm each. I had had a word with myself and managed to calm myself down slightly despite being petrified so complied and got out of the van with no dramas. I knew enough to know what would happen to me should I kick off or resist and I had already witnessed that despite being an officer myself I was treated no different to Joe public – in fact I was treated with no respect or compassion at all.

The usual routine would be that a person would be taken to the custody desk and presented before the custody sergeant, however I skipped that process and was taken straight to a cell. The realisation hit me again of where I was and I went into fight or flight mode again and started screaming and crying which panicked the officers and again I was thrown into the cell onto the concrete floor and the door slammed behind me and the little hatch slid up so I couldn't see out. My handcuffs had been taken off me quickly during this and the cut from the cuff on my left wrist was now bleeding and was stinging badly. I pulled myself up to my knees and placed myself in the corner of the cell in a ball like position rocking forward and backwards trying to calm myself down whilst sobbing like I'd never sobbed before.

Every now and again the little hatch in the door slid down and I could see a face on the other side checking on me, checking that I was behaving myself. Sometimes I think it was just so-called colleagues of mine coming to have a look at their colleague, the officer who had been arrested and lying vulnerable in a cell in her PJs. I still remember the giggling on the other side of the door as if I was some kind of freak show that they had paid to see. It then slid up and I was left alone again with just the mumbling of voices outside and the banging of doors from the other neighbours. Eventually I heard the sound of keys rattling and the door swung open. There stood an officer and two women. The same two women that had been in my home about an hour earlier before I was carted off. What made them think I would even entertain them now when I didn't earlier in my safe place. I blamed them for letting the police officers take me. They entered the cell and muttered some words but I still don't know to this day what they were. I presume they were outlining what was going to happen to me next as I was soon to be moved from the cell to an ambulance in company with a police officer. I don't know if it was ignorance or the fact that my brain had completely crashed that I still hadn't come to the conclusion that I was on my way to hospital and that the nightmare that I was in was about to get a lot worse.

CHAPTER FIVE

Again, the journey seemed to take forever. It was dark outside by this point and I had no idea where I was going due to the tiny window in the ambulance being too high to see out of. We eventually came to a stop and the officer said to me that it was time to go. There was a bit of a sympathetic look in her eyes, the first sign of any compassion that I had had since I'd been removed from my home. She took hold of my hand and told me not to worry and that everything would be okay. It wasn't much but it meant so much to me that someone had treated me with a bit of respect.

I climbed out of the ambulance and into the cold air outside where a tall guy was waiting. The officer exchanged a few words with him and handed him some paperwork and the two of them took me into the building in front of me which was to be my new home for the next four weeks. It was hard to see what the building looked like but I remember it being very old and creepy looking, like something you would see out of a film many years ago where they took the troubled and vulnerable who were never to be seen again. I was relatively calm at this point as I genuinely believed I would just be having a chat with someone and then my mum and dad would pick me up and take me home. How wrong was I. I was led into a small room that just contained three chairs and the male asked me if I would like a drink which I declined. I didn't want anything from these strangers until I knew exactly what was going on. I may have lost the plot but I knew I had to keep my wits about me and for all I knew they could pop anything into a drink without me knowing. The officer was still with me at this point and explained that she needed to stay a while longer. We sat there for what seemed like an eternity and eventually two more people came into the room. They sat down, introduced themselves and I haven't got a clue who they were to this day, and then basically went on to say that I was in hospital and was being detained under a section 2 order of the Mental Health Act. I could feel the blood draining out of me and the room started to spin and my anxiety levels were going off the scale.

Despite my state of mind at this point I knew what that meant. It meant I was being kept against my will for up to four weeks in hospital for assessment. My rights and freedom stripped from me in an instant. I didn't give myself chance to tell myself to stay calm and instead went straight into panic mode and completely flipped. Not out of anything other than shear panic. I wasn't violent in any way, I just wanted out of that room and building and away from these people that were trying to hold me against my will. I made a run for the door in front of me but only got a few steps before the officer took me to the floor and before I knew it, I was back in cuffs, the left one digging harder and harder into the small cut from the last time they were applied. I kept screaming for her to get off me and that all I wanted was to go home. They knew I was no threat to them but I suppose they couldn't take any chances and were just doing their job at the end of the day just as I had done over and over again when I attended these types of incidents.

Whilst lying on the floor more and more people entered the room to help the officer as I was wriggling about trying to escape her grip. There were four of them now, one on each of my limbs, and before I knew it was being carried out of the room and down a long echoey corridor where all I could hear were my screams and sobbing and the pleading with them to let me go. I distinctly remember the smell of fresh paint, later discovering the white walls had to be regularly redecorated because they were stained with blood or scrawled pen marks. No one spoke a word and I was carried through a large door ahead of me that was being held open by a female wearing some kind of uniform. I was carried past her and again down another corridor, hearing the door bang behind me and the sound of keys locking the big metal door. Realisation suddenly hit me. I was on a ward, in a psychiatric hospital with some very unwell patients, me being one of them.

It was hard to get my bearings as I was currently lying face down with my head pushed to one side and what felt like a heard of elephants sat on my back and two people one on either side of me pinning my arms to the floor attempting to stop me getting up. Yes, I was lashing out and screaming but only because I was absolutely petrified, not for any reason other than the fact that struggling to get out of this situation is also a survival mechanism, in fact no one would be pinned down without struggling. I remember saying please get off me I can't breathe and told them that I would calm down, but no one moved and I was shoved further and further into the dirty grey carpet beneath me. It was that thin cheap carpet that wears away under your feet and plucks at the slightest thing. It was that thin it was almost transparent; I saw no use for it and they might as well have left the floor bare. It had a musty smell to it like it had been there years and years and had many a patients feet trodden on it or face pushed into it.

Next minute I remember a sharp pain in one of my upper legs near my buttocks. It was a strange feeling as no sooner had I felt it I was starting to get a weird sensation throughout my entire body and all my anger and fear started to slowly slip away. I remember lying there thinking what was that sharp pain I felt and then reality hit. One of them had injected me with something and it must have been something strong as the effect it had on me was so quick and effective, so much so that one by one they climbed off my back and loosened their grips on my arms. I had been pumped with enough sedatives 'to knock a horse out'. As I lay there heavy breathing like I'd just run a marathon, I can clearly remember the sound of someone being sick and crying. I am unsure to this day whether it was another patient or even a member of staff who maybe couldn't cope with the amount of force that had just been used on me, a scared, vulnerable female. Or maybe they were new at this role and this had been their first experience of witnessing such aggressive and unjustified behaviour. This is something that has always stuck in my head and I guess I will never get the answer. It's proven that restraint can have a significant psychological effect on everyone involved, including those that witness it.

MHAA (Mental Health Act Assessment) Guidelines set out the principle that restraint should only be used, when necessary, justifiable and proportionate to the perceived threat and although I was not completely compliant, I still don't believe that any of these can be applied to this situation or any other situations that was to follow over the next twenty-eight days. Surely, they must have known that I was just scared and treating me in this manner would have only made me worse.

I was left on the floor face down, on that dirty grey carpet, for what seemed like an eternity and although I was completely out of it, I could still see people out of the corner of my eye going about their usual business laughing and joking between themselves. I was still hoping I was having a very bad nightmare and was going to wake up at any moment. However, I didn't, this was real, this was happening. I think they were waiting for me to be completely lifeless like a fish that had just been caught and hit over the head, before they moved me and when that time came a couple of staff came over to me and carried me a short distance into a small room with a bed and placed me on it. This was to be my new bedroom for the next four weeks. I was left in my pjs that were stuck to me with sweat through the sheer terror of the brutal way they had just treated me and the door closed behind me with a bang. It wasn't locked but I knew from the force it was shut that I wasn't to get up and try and open it, I daren't move after what had just happened to me. I lay there thinking I'm going to die in this place and for the next hour tried my best to control my sobbing so not to make a sound and give these people any reason to return to my room tonight. I must have finally drifted off to sleep as when I next opened my eyes it was daylight. Day one I thought of my twenty-eight day sentence. A sentence I had been given for being poorly and not understood. I felt like I was being punished and told off for being naughty when, in reality, I was really unwell.

During my time in hospital, I was very weak and underweight. I'm not particularly tall but not short either, about 5'7" and weighed under eight stone, which was light for me as I had always been around the nine stone mark. I knew this as I'd stepped on the scales at home not long before being taken away. My athletic figure that I was once so proud of through all my exercise and hard work had turned into me looking withdrawn, especially in the face where my cheeks had become even more prominent, to the point they looked sunken. I was never a violent patient: a little stubborn and eccentric, maybe, but mostly just terrified, not in any kind of position to do anyone any harm. So, when the staff on the ward grabbed me, or slammed me against a wall, wrestling me to the floor, in my delusional state, they were not just hurting me, they were killing me inside. It was not just like a little jostling: in those moments, it felt very much like my life was coming to an end. With each push, shove or grab, I was slowly losing myself.

CHAPTER SIX

The sun shone through the bars on my window, there were no curtains to block out the light as it hit every bar and the far wall of my room. I was still dressed in the same pjs that I left my home in less than twenty-four hours earlier. I slowly pulled myself up and swung my legs to the side of the bed, still a bit dazed from last night's episode. I scanned my room, if you can call it that. More like something that had been thrown together, obviously completely suicidal proof. No hangers in the wardrobe just shelves, a small chair in the corner of the room that was stuck to the floor so I wasn't able to move it. Next to that a small sink. That was it. No mirror for obvious reasons. I just sat there staring out of the window through the bars. I might as well have been taken to a prison. I tried to convince myself though that this was a hospital, hospitals are a place of safety where people cared and where people were brought to get well. How wrong was I and the next month more than proved that this place was not set up to help me but mentally torture me day by day.

I slowly got off my bed, bare footed, and walked over to the window and looked out. Despite the iron bars I could still feel the sun on my face, it felt warm, comforting in a way. My room looked out onto a grassed area below and a small wooden bench to the left. There was no one about but I wasn't sure what time it was as there was no clock in my room and I faintly remember my watch being taken off me in the police station. I walked round my room which literally took five seconds as it was that small. It was then that I heard the sound of footsteps in the distance which got louder and louder before they stopped outside my room. Oh God please don't open the door, please don't come into my room. I was terrified they were going to hurt me or put that poison in my body again so that I wouldn't be a problem to them. The door swung open and a woman in what appeared to be some kind of nurse's uniform stood in the doorway. It wasn't your traditional nurse's uniform, just a pale blue short sleeved top and blue pants. More like the kind you'd see staff wearing in a care home. The only difference being the NHS logo printed in small print on the front.

"Good morning" The female said. "Did you sleep well?" then informing me that it was 9am. Sleep well? Was this woman having a laugh. Did she not know I was knocked out with something that basically put me into a coma. I felt like I had to acknowledge her so as to avoid any conflict and to be honest I was still trying to suss out how I needed to behave in this place in order to survive.

I just nodded my head in a gesture to reply yes. No sooner had I done this that she came over to me holding out a little white pot made of paper and I quickly saw that it had white tablets in of different sizes. She explained to me that it was my daily medication and that if I wanted to get better, I needed to comply and take the medication that was offered to me. I had no other option than to trust this professional person stood in front of me, and to be fair this was the first time since being taken away that someone had mentioned the word 'get better'. I later discovered that these tablets weren't given to me to help me or make me better in any way. They were merely poured down my throat to supress that last bit of any rational thinking, emotion or independence I had and I was to discover this over the next few days to come as I slipped more and more into a vegetated state.

The woman asked me to stick out my tongue after I put the pills in my mouth, just for that reassurance that I had swallowed them which I had. She then left the room returning straight away with a small pile of clothes in her hands which I immediately recognised to be mine. Did that mean that someone was here in this very building that I knew, a loved one. Were they here to rescue me from this hell hole. If I shouted loud enough, would they burst into my room and whisk me away. The answer was no as the woman then explained that a police officer had dropped me some personal belongings off. Personal I thought as I starred at the pile of clothes with a toothbrush, toothpaste and hairbrush on top. Was this it? No photographs of my family, or letters. She popped the clothes on one of the shelves in the miniature wardrobe and told me to get ready explaining that I would be going for a bath. What she didn't explain was that this bath involved a member of staff being present throughout it. I couldn't even be trusted to bathe myself and that first bath on my first morning there, was the quickest bath that I have ever had. As I got in, the water on my left wrist immediately started to sting and I remembered about the cut that had been left by the handcuffs, the trauma flooding back in an instance. As I stared down at my wrist there was about an inch long deep cut in bedded in my wrist.

I quickly washed and splashed the water on my face time and time again. A supervisor at work once told me at the start of my breakdown that when she was going through a tough time, she always found it helpful to hold her face in the shower for a while or splash water on it. I found the whole concept of it silly at the time but right at the moment when I was doing it, I got it, it helped. It was as though for that split second my thoughts disappeared. I still do it to this day and find it comforting.

I was escorted back to my room and finally given a bit of time on my own, the door being left slightly ajar. I was advised that when I was ready, I could go into the dining room and get breakfast. No way was I eating anything in here I thought. However, I wasn't going to stare at the walls of my bedroom all day so I built up the courage to leave my room and entered the bland echoey corridor with its white washed walls. I had no idea where I was going but just headed towards the sound of clanging plates and chit a chatter and presumed, I was heading in the right direction. I got to the door, peered in, and the room was filled with long dining tables and people, some in that nurse's uniform and some dressed like me who I presumed were the other inmates. A member of staff came over to me and encouraged me to sit down at one of the tables. She then asked if I wanted anything to eat and I just nodded and said yes please. I was scared to eat but at the same time felt a bit hungry as I hadn't eaten for what seemed like days. She placed the bland toast and butter down in front of me and a cup of water in a plastic beaker. I took a bite and quickly realised that I wasn't hungry after all as I still had that sickly feeling and a knot in my stomach. Anxiety can do weird things to your body.

I picked at the toast and by the time I decided I didn't want to eat the dining hall had emptied and there was just me and the member of staff left in there. I told her I wanted to go back to my room and got up. She didn't follow me so I presumed I was given my first bit of independence and instead of going straight back to my room started to explore my new residence. I exited the dining room door back onto the echoey corridor and at the end of it was the big metal door that I had been carried through in a petrified state the day before. I slowly walked down it and, on the left, there was a panel of glass to a room that appeared to be the communal area and observed a TV in the corner, a sofa and a couple of large chairs. Beyond this room there was a telephone attached to the wall and next to that another door that was closed with a small panel of glass in the top. I could see a number of people crammed into a tiny room wearing those nurse's uniforms. There were numerous shelves to the left that were filled with plastic boxes upon boxes of medication. There was a large clock mounted to the wall above the door. Opposite that room was a radiator underneath a large window that looked out onto a carpark below. I sat on the radiator for a while and just stared out of the window watching the world go by outside, envious of the people coming and going of their own free will and not locked in a building. You take these things for granted until they're suddenly taken away from you.

CHAPTER SEVEN

I sat there contemplating how much my life had changed and how I was ever going to get out of this place. Before I knew it, I got lost in my thoughts and when I glanced over to the large clock, I realised I had actually been sat on that radiator for the majority of the day. I guess that's what a combination of medication and trauma does for you. The medication that was given to me earlier that morning had well and truly kicked in and if anything, it had placed me in a calm place. I was still petrified but was starting to feel that numb that I wanted to go with that feeling for the time being as it felt safer. I heard someone shout tea is being served and couldn't believe I'd been sat there that long that I'd missed lunch. I got up and walked back towards the dining room and tried to eat a little, again forcing myself as I still felt so sick. I was starting to feel tired now so decided to go back to my room for a bit of a lie down. I hadn't spoken to anyone all day, not even the other patients. I'd clocked a few that were intrigued with the new girl on the block but tried not to make eye contact. I think my main concern was any of them finding out I was a police officer. I get that this place was a hospital of some sort but I was wise enough to realise that these places also attracted the kind of people that as a police officer you tended to have the pleasure of dealing with which in turn meant you weren't their biggest fan.

I was woken up by someone shaking me gently and when I opened my eyes the room was dark and the only light coming in was that from the corridor. I couldn't believe I'd slept so long again. They were stood over me holding that little paper pot and pushed it towards me. More tablets I thought, I only had some this morning. However, it was easier to just take them than question it or refuse so I placed them in my mouth taking a sip of water to ensure it was safely deposited. They then left the room. I remember closing my eyes thinking that I had survived my first day locked up and my freedom stripped of me and then suddenly got that gut wrenching feeling in my stomach again when I realised, I had a least another twenty-seven days to go and believe you me today was a breeze compared to what was to come.

I'll skip forward now to the end of the week as week one was pretty much the same every day. Wake up, get escorted to the bathroom, get escorted back to my room, given my cocktail of meds, breakfast in the dining room, sat on my radiator looking out of the big window, tea, more meds, bed, repeat! That was basically it the first week. I kept myself to myself and observed the different patients coming and going, some more poorly than others, some scarier than others. However, a handful were the same faces throughout. One face in particular stood out to me that week. A female with short hair who had a permanent scowl on her face. I could tell she wasn't my biggest fan and wasn't quite sure why until one day she came up to me and asked if 'I was the filth' Her voice was very deep and no specific accent that I could pin point. I denied it as much as I could but what was the point, she knew, how, I had no idea but this girl was soon to become my worst nightmare. Every time I walked past her, she made it quite clear she knew and the looks and threats became a daily occurrence. I didn't think I could feel any more scared but I was, I now feared for my safety not only from the staff but now another patient.

The days felt like they stretched on forever as there was nothing to do. You might think you'd receive intensive therapy whilst inside, but in all honesty, I never received any therapy or the offer of it throughout the whole of my time in there. Each day I started to feel more and more out of it. I'm guessing that was the cocktail of medication that they pumped into me twice a day. I had shown no signs of violence nor agitation since day one so I couldn't understand why they were trying to numb me so much and make me lose all senses completely. Yes, I felt calm but I was also losing me, more and more. Through naivety I always thought these places were supposed to offer talking therapy, get to the root of your problem and even fix you. After all I still thought I was dying but couldn't rationalise why, I was in desperate need of help but no offer of it came. I quickly realised that all they were for was to lock you in and drug you up and if you didn't comply, you'd know about it. I knew that if I was to survive in this place, I had to stop taking this medication somehow in order to keep a clear mind and keep my wits about me, so that is what I decided to do. The big question was how was I going to do it without getting caught as big brother was permanently watching over me. I needed to think about this carefully and not be too quick to act on it as there was no way I was being pinned to the floor again like when I was admitted. I wasn't going to give them the satisfaction. I was going to sleep on it and have a serious think. In fact, sleeping was the only thing I seemed to do in the first week, partly to block out my surroundings but also as a result of the medication.

CHAPTER EIGHT

I woke up again to a different member of staff standing over my bed. I hadn't seen her before but she seemed pleasant enough and greeted me with good morning before thrusting the little paper pot in front of my face and handing me a plastic cup with water in. Medication time she said. I decided today was definitely the day to stop taking this poison so I popped it in my mouth and quickly shoved the tablets to the inside of my cheeks and took a tiny sip of water and pretended to swallow them. Unlike the other staff, luckily, she didn't ask me to open my mouth and stick out my tongue and left the room pretty sharply as one of the alarms had gone off in one of the other rooms. My plan couldn't have gone better. I quickly spat the tablets out into my hand and scanned the room looking for somewhere to stash them so no one could find them. It was hard as the room was so bare so I just placed them under my mattress for now until I could think of somewhere else to put them. I still felt completely out of it and numb but I felt better already knowing that this was the start of getting these drugs out of my system. This was me, getting control of my life again.

Another day, same routine. Got dressed, breakfast and then back to my perch on the radiator to watch the comings and goings of the world outside. I asked one of the staff coming out of the office how long I had been here as I honestly had no idea. She told me that today was day six and in my calculation I had just over three weeks left in this hell hole. She told me that my mum and dad were coming to visit me tomorrow. I just nodded and turned my head away from her and for the first time in a long time I could feel the corners of my mouth turn upwards. I was actually managing to smile which was probably a grimace, but felt good anyway as I hadn't managed anything near this in a very, very, long time. Surely, they could get me out of this place, they were my parents, they could do anything. The good news gave me a bit of energy and I jumped off the radiator and decided to take a walk to the communal lounge across the corridor and watch a bit of TV to pass a bit more of the day. The couches were already taken up so I sat on a wooden chair and stared blankly at the screen having no idea or retaining what I was watching. I scanned the room quickly and every person in there had that blank expression and looked drugged up to the eyeballs, everyone except that girl. The girl that kept staring at me intensely making the hairs on my arms stand up. The one that in her words knew I was

'The Filth', the one that had made sly remarks every time I saw her in the corridor or sitting down for tea. I quickly realised I wasn't welcome in there and stood up and left the room and decided to go and have a lie down for a while in my room. I must have fallen asleep as soon as I hit the pillow as before I knew it, I was being woken up again and offered a banana shake at the same time being informed that I had missed lunch. She handed me the shake and my medication. She didn't even stay this time to watch me put it in my mouth and left the room. Surely trust couldn't have been built this quickly but I went with it and slipped the pills straight out of the pot and under my mattress. The relief that I didn't even have to put them in my mouth was immense. My plan was actually working, or so I thought.

Although I slept most of the afternoon, I still felt really groggy so decided to just stay in my room and rest and for the next couple of hours I stared blankly at the ceiling trying to figure out what had gone so wrong in my life to end up in this place. I was quickly shaken out of my thoughts by the loud bell that echoed the corridor that meant tea was ready. I wasn't hungry in the slightest but dragged myself to the dining room. It was easier that way than to get preached at about keeping my strength up. I picked at my food and pushed it around my plate and then went back to my room. I thought if I could sleep, tomorrow would come quicker and I would get to see my lovely mum and dad. My meds arrived and luckily, I was able to conceal them again as she left the room. A whole day without any tablets. I didn't feel any better yet and knew it had taken time to get in my system so figured it must take time to leave it so I realised I had to be patient.

Tomorrow couldn't have come quick enough as that day was the day, I got to see my mum and dad. They were the only people that were allowed to come and visit me. I since learnt that my ex-partner was told not to visit me as it may hinder my recovery. I beg to differ as I would have done anything to see her at the time. I didn't get excited about anything these days but the thought of seeing my parents, hugging them and basically seeing a friendly face gave me butterflies. I was hoping they would have all the answers and even be able to get me out today and take me home. I had so many unanswered questions and parents knew everything, or so I thought. I managed to swerve my meds again that morning but still wasn't feeling any different and still had that zombie feeling, however decided to just go with it and enjoy the fact that I would be around them and couldn't wait to feel their arms wrapped round me. I was told that they would be arriving about 2pm and given that it was only 10am now, the next four hours seemed more like forty hours. I sat on my radiator staring out in the hope that they might be early. The hands on the clock above the office going round and round in slow motion.

Eventually it got to 1.45pm and a member of staff came up to me and asked me to return to my room, explaining that this was the routine when visitors came. I guessed they wanted to speak to my parents alone quickly and update them on my condition, I was going to say progress but that would be lying as I hadn't had any offer of any help since being admitted, only the mandatory drugs. I went back to my room as instructed and waited patiently and eventually I was collected and escorted towards the visiting room opposite the office. As I got to the door, I peered through the glass panel and could see my mum and dad sat in the corner of the room on two plastic chairs. I pushed the door open that quickly that it bounced off the wall and I ran up to my mum flinging my arms around her neck and squeezing her that tightly that I didn't want to ever let go. It wasn't long before I felt my mum's tears on my cheek and slowly loosened my grip around her neck and stepped back slightly to see her withdrawn, tired face and the worry and stress in her eyes. She asked me if I was okay but I felt as though it should be me asking her. My dad made a nervous coughing sound and I walked towards him and gave him the same reassuring hug that I needed, and then sat down. The door had been shut to by now but I could see a member of staff though the glass panel standing outside like they were acting as a bouncer at a night club. What did they think was going to happen for Gods' sake, I was with my mum and dad. I hadn't caused any issues since day one when I was brought in here and I certainly wasn't going to start now and risk my visit being cut short.

My mum asked me if I had been eating which was her polite way of saying that I had lost far too much weight.

I told her I had but didn't have much appetite but was eating enough so not to worry. It was strange as I didn't really have anything to talk about as every day had been the same for the last seven days. The only bit of news I had was how they treated me when I arrived and the horrific way, they dealt with me and how scared I was of the girl who called me filth. Both of these bits of news I didn't want to bother them with, as much as I wanted to. They looked ill and worried enough and I didn't want to put any more worry on them at this time. I asked them if they had been told about the future plans for me and whether I could get out any sooner. They had been told the same though, that I was under a section 2 order and would be assessed after twenty-eight days which meant I had another three weeks left in here at least. I still felt really out of it and although I was engaging in conversation, I wasn't retaining anything that my mum and dad were speaking about other than that I was here for another twenty-one days.

Prior to entering the room, I was told that I only had thirty minutes with them which I thought was ridiculous. However as much as I didn't want to feel it, I felt that it was more than enough as I couldn't bear to see the look of hurt, worry and stress on their faces a minute more than I had to. I felt so guilty and responsible for their hurt and pain that I almost felt it unbearable. The woman stood on guard outside quickly popped her head in to inform us that we only had five minutes left. I decided to use these five minutes to try and reassure them that I was okay as best as I could but as much as I tried, I knew that they didn't believe me, they were my parents, my flesh and blood. They could see how scared I was as I could them and although we were all thinking the same thing, we just spent the last few minutes in silence just hugging each other and crying. I didn't want the time to end as it was the safest, I'd felt for a week. The woman popped back in and told us that the time was up and to finish our conversation. I gave them both another hug and as I started walking out of the room my mum grabbed hold of my arm and pulled me back towards her and whispered in my ear "Everything is going to be okay, I promise". I attempted a half-hearted smile and squeezed her hand as I left the room. I was screaming inside and wanted to bolt for the door and make a run for it but not only was I too tired and drugged up, I knew it would do me no favours and I wanted them to come back next week.

CHAPTER NINE

I lay in my room that night, still scared and anxious but a little bit of me felt content and I'm guessing that was from seeing my mum and dad. It may have been brief and full of silences but those silences brought me comfort and I was counting down the days till my next visit next Sunday. I stayed in my room for the majority of the day with the routine visits of the staff breaking my silence offering me my drugs which I was still able to hide and avoid taking. It was now day three of no poison in my system and although I still felt the effects, I felt a little bit more in control of my body and had a bit of my independence back, or so I thought.

I was woken up the next day to not one but three members of staff stood over my bed. I quickly tried to rack my brains for a reason there were so many, or if I had done something wrong yesterday to annoy them but I couldn't. One of the staff then stepped forward and thrust the little all familiar paper pot in front of my face and said "Now are you going to be a good girl and take these or are you going to hide them under your mattress with the rest of your stash". I felt the blood rush to my head and the constant knot in my stomach get tighter as if someone had climbed in it and tied a rope round it and was pulling it with every bit of strength they had from every angle. Since being a child, I had never been any good at lying and my face always gave it away so I didn't think it was worth even trying to, or even come up with an excuse as these weren't the kind of people to listen let alone understand.

Before I had the chance to respond the female whipped back the covers and the man behind her stepped forward and pulled up the corner of my mattress revealing a pile of tablets stuck to the mattress. All three of them had that disapproving angry look on their faces which I had witnessed many times during the last week. How the hell did they know I hadn't been taking them and more importantly how did they know I had hidden them there. I always made sure the staff had left the room before I even spat the tablets out into my hand. There was only one way, my room must have a camera in it somewhere and despite this being fifteen years ago I honestly thought human rights existed back then and there were rules for this kind of thing and privacy was in place for even these kinds of situations. I had to ask the question but none of them replied, why would they. They probably thought I was too docile to even think of this let alone build up the courage to ask them. I knew I was right but didn't push the conversation so just concentrated on what was to come. The female pushed the white pot closer towards my face and said "It's your choice. You either take these or we will forcibly make you take them". They didn't even give me time to reply or respond to their requests. The female stood behind her then raised her left hand and there it was, that same needle that had been used on day one, and presumably the same poison inside it that left me paralysed. I can still remember the sharp prick of the needle in my thigh and that feeling of slipping away into near unconsciousness and loss of control. This is something that I wasn't risking happening again, this needle of doom was coming nowhere near my body. Why were they treating me like this? Yes, I had gone against them with my medication but for good reason but no one even attempted to talk to me in a calm manner or reason with me, just straight to the level of threats.

As much as I didn't want to take the tablets again, I also didn't want to be forcibly held down and restrained so I put my hand out and grabbed the white pot off her, throwing the tablets into my mouth. The woman behind her handed me a cup of water and told me to wash the tablets down immediately or there would be trouble. For a spilt second, I debated whether to slide them to the corner of mouth and conceal them but what was the point, there was no way they were leaving my room until they knew I had swallowed them so that is what I did. Back to square one and back on the road to feeling like a zombie and no control again. Once I stuck my tongue out and opened my mouth wide, they were satisfied that they had gone and then left me room, one of them muttering that I better not try that trick again. I lay on my bed completely deflated and also on guard as I was convinced that I was being watched twenty-four seven. I was paranoid enough prior to being committed to this place so this was only going to make my situation worse. I couldn't believe that the last few days had been a complete waste of time and the tablets would soon be back in my system supressing every bit of emotion that I had left. Not only that, I knew that I would be watched like a hawk from now on which made me even more anxious.

CHAPTER TEN

Monday morning arrived, the start of week two and the start to my half way mark of being in here before I get to escape. Since being caught out yesterday with my tablets, the staff seemed even more cold and robotic than before. The next couple of days to come were nothing to report and I basically kept my head down and stayed in my room as much as I could. That scary girl had been sniffing around a bit and started with the digs again but I didn't have the energy to entertain her but at the same time tried to keep my wits about me and keep out of her way. It was stepping up a notch to be fair and the odd occasional snide comment had turned into her nudging me with her shoulder as we passed each other in the corridor. It was nothing too aggressive so she wasn't seen, but at the same time it was enough to make me fall off balance ever so slightly and make it known that she really did not like me and to watch my back.

It got to Wednesday and it was the same old boring day stuck in this prehistoric building whilst the sun shone outside. I always loved the outdoors and would give anything to be out there right now going for my daily run and feeling that warmth of the sun on my cheeks. However, I was told last week that I had to earn my trust with them before they would let me step outside the main door which was ridiculous in itself. I was a police officer. For God's sake, I may not be wearing that uniform at the moment but I still was one on paper and would hopefully be able to wear that uniform again someday however unrealistic that felt at the time. The majority of that morning I sat on my little perch outside the main office staring out of the window in a daydream. The only interaction I had was the staff giving me my lunchtime meds and making me drink some milkshake thing that they said was full of nutrients. To be fair I knew I had lost a lot of weight as my clothes were hanging off me but I didn't see the point in eating anymore, I was starting to give up completely and at meal times I either skipped or pushed the food around my plate. I think this was a combination of not being hungry through the stress and anxiety of everything but also this was the one thing, the only thing, that I had control over as everything else had been taken away from me. I decided whether I would eat that day not them. That is why I was being asked to take these shakes as they knew I was rebelling a bit and they had to be seen to be looking after me despite this being so far from reality.

I'm going to skip forward to the Saturday and the day that things took a drastic and unimaginable turn. Up until now, yes, my time in here had been horrendous and the worst two weeks of my life, however my time from this day forward was about to get a lot worse. I knew my parents would be visiting me on the Sunday and I didn't want to be dosed up again so that I could barely string a sentence together so decided to hide my meds again. This time not in my room as I knew it was covered by a camera but instead in a little gap in the wall where I sat on the radiator. I was given my meds there at lunchtime and I managed to do my old trick of pretending to swallow them but this time gave it a while before I spat them out. I started out of the window for about ten minutes with the tablets stuck to the inside of my cheeks, trying not to swallow or let them dissolve in my mouth.

When I thought it was safe to do so I pretended to sneeze into a tissue and at the same time spat them out gently into the tissue paper, rolling it up afterwards and leaving it a while until the coast was clear, then stuffing it into a tiny gap between the radiator and the wall. I knew I only had twenty-four hours before my parents were due to visit but I didn't want any more medication pumped into my system before then. However, this was the worst mistake I had made so far since being in here. About an hour later three members of staff came up to me and asked me to take the medication from out behind the radiator. How stupid and naïve of me to think that the corridors didn't have cameras on too, if they can spy on you in your own bedroom then they're definitely going to spy on you in the communal areas.

Before I even had chance to speak let alone get the tissue paper out, one of the staff members, a female I think, grabbed hold of my arm and pulled me off the radiator onto the floor shouting "This has got to stop you silly girl". I attempted to shrug her off as she still had hold of the top of my arm with a strong enough grip that I could feel it, however this only made the situation worse as it gave them an excuse to think I was going to be aggressive which I wasn't. They only needed the slightest excuse to act on it, which I'm sure they loved to do. Before I knew it there were about five members of staff surrounding me which sent me into panic mode as I had no idea what was going to happen next. Another member of staff took hold of my other arm and the female in front of me said that I needed to go with them. Go where I thought, what the hell were they going to do with me now? and I really didn't want to find out so I went into flight mode and tried to get away from them. Where I was going to go, I had no idea as there was nowhere to hide in this place, but I knew I needed to do something. I didn't stand a chance though as all five members of staff pounced on me and took me to the floor again like they were playing a game of rugby. I lashed out as much as I could but my energy wore out quickly and I was soon dragged along the long corridor by my feet like a lamb being taken to the slaughter, no dignity or humanity about it in the slightest.

Could they not see that I was just a scared girl and needed a bit of compassion, not a threat to them in any way shape or form. It seemed like an eternity being dragged along that polished white floor and all I could hear were my screams again echoing against the walls like they had on day one when I was admitted, and all the laughter of the staff as if it was some sort of game. They were actually enjoying treating a vulnerable scared girl in this way. We were heading back towards my room but instead of turning right we turned left and then another sudden left turn through a metal door that was being held open by someone. I then heard the slam of the door and the sound of keys rattling and soon realised I was locked in but not on my own, with the five members of staff that had dragged me there. I lay on the floor for a minute or two panting and out of breath from the shear shock of being dragged and treated in this manner. I can recall some of the staff leaning against the wall trying to compose themselves for what was about to come. I still had no idea what this was going to be as no one had said a word to me. Two of them then stepped forward and scooped me up from behind and lifted me into a chair that was placed in the corner of the bare room, in fact that was the only thing in there, no windows or any other furniture.

The two of them that picked me up kept held of my arms pinning them down to the chair which they had managed to recline slightly so that I was now lying back on a slant. A male then walked round the back of the chair and grabbed hold of my head holding it back on the head rest, another stepping forward and placing a knee on my chest, applying slight pressure to my sternum. This left the other female present, free to do what was to come next which was horrendous and makes me feel sick to this day. I genuinely thought my life was over as the level of force and aggression that they were all using was disgusting. The female stepped forward and I quickly caught a glance of numerous tablets in her hand and a bottle of water in her other hand. The male that had hold of my head told me to open my mouth and before I had chance to ask why he told me that if I was going to hide my medication then this would be the consequence. He then shoved my head back with force, and during the screams for help from myself the female managed to lock open my mouth with her hand and shove the tablets right down my throat with her fingers. She shoved them that far down and with that much force that I could feel her nails scratching on my skin on the inside of my throat. I attempted to get her away from me but it was impossible with the other two restraining my arms and the male kneeling on my chest, which he had now applied more pressure to and it was starting to restrict my breathing slightly. Not forgetting the male that had my head pinned back. I wasn't going anywhere but I wasn't letting them think that this was right and continued to struggle but there was no use as those tablets, whatever they were, were going down my throat whether I liked it or not as the female then put the bottle of water up to my mouth and continued to tip it down my throat until I was choking.

I felt like I was drowning and couldn't breathe as the male kneeling on my chest got heavier and the water just kept coming and coming and before I knew, it was all over me. I couldn't believe what was happening and how vile they were treating me. This went on for about five minutes and when they eventually stopped it took me a while to catch my breath and calm down, both from the drowning and choking sensation and the shear panic. In the mean time they had all climbed off me, loosening their grip one by one and as they did so I caught a glimpse of the finger marks they had left on my arm which had already started to go red. This was a reminder of how much force they had actually used. What made it even more degrading and traumatising was the sound of laughter and joking between them, as if they had actually enjoyed what had just happened. It felt so degrading to be dealt with in this manner, especially by supposed 'Professionals', people that were meant to have chosen that profession to care for people and make them better. Not traumatise them even more and treat them like a piece of meat.

I lay there for a while in a lonely dark vacant room as they all left immediately after, locking the door behind them. I lay there in complete exhaustion and shock over what had just taken place. I may have been very poorly, but I knew that what had just happened to me was a straight up assault. As a police officer I have undergone rigorous and regular training in correct restraint and the correct level of restraint, and more importantly when restraint is proportionate and absolutely necessary. This was definitely not the case in this particular situation. That feeling of shock soon turned into a feeling of dismay and calmness as the tablets soon started to kick in and before I knew it, I had crawled onto the floor and was lying there on that all familiar dirty grey carpet panting like a dog just staring and fixated on the wall in front of me that was just as drab and dirty as the carpet. Every part of me felt numb and not one fraction of me felt any emotion as the tablets had given me that numbness and loss of self- control as they always did, however this time even more so. I figured they must have stepped the medication up a notch. I lay there for what felt like an eternity but in reality, was probably only about thirty minutes or so when I heard the keys rattling on the other side of the door. Two members of staff then entered the room. They didn't require an army of them now, they had sedated me enough so I could barely move let alone thrash out at them in fear. They picked me up by each arm, not uttering one word as they escorted me back to my room. I felt like I was walking on clouds and at peace from the hell that I had endured less than thirty minutes ago. I was placed on my bed and they left my room shutting my door behind them. I wanted to scream and cry hysterically, and inside I was but I couldn't show that what had just happened had hurt and scared me in ways that I can't even fully put into words still to this day. I also felt that if I showed any emotion then they would see this as a weakness and that the next time as I was sure there would be a next time, would be even worse! I lay back on my bed and must have literally passed out as soon as my head hit the pillow.

CHAPTER ELEVEN

I was glad when I woke early the next morning to discover that it was Sunday and my parents would be visiting me. I would be able to tell them exactly what happened yesterday and surely when they knew the truth, they would be able to get me out of this place. I may have lost my mind slightly but even I knew that what happened was unjustified and quite frankly immoral. It was a straight up assault on myself. That morning consisted of me doing as I was told, breakfast and meds, and then I decided to wait outside in the corridor for them to arrive. Watching them through the window, pull into the carpark made me feel that bit more of security and comfort for those extra minutes before they arrived on the ward. It was now 10am and I was told that the visit had been arranged for 11am.

Only an hour to pass and the truth could be told and I would finally be saved. How wrong was I though. Just as I had done my last clock check at 10.15am a member of staff came up to me holding the all-familiar white paper pot. I'd already had my morning meds so panic had instantly kicked in at the dread of what they were trying to give me now. The female stretched out her arm pushing the paper pot towards me. I expected there to be a cocktail of drugs but instead was one tiny blue pill sitting at the bottom all alone. I asked what it was and that I had never taken anything this colour before as all my other drugs were white. I expected some explanation but all I got was that she had been asked to give it me. Asked? By whom? I thought, and I demanded an explanation but the only reply I got was that if I didn't take it before my parents arrived then the visit would be cancelled.

Looking back on it now, it was so obvious why they were giving me this but at the time I had no idea. In short, this little blue pill when swallowed took about twenty minutes for it to take effect which basically turned me into a zombie. No emotion, no memory of anything (including the previous day) and no ability to hold any type of conversation other than the odd nod of the head. Yes, they were basically drugging me up so I remained silent and unable to tell the horrific events that happened to me on the Saturday. I still don't know what this pill was or was made up of but considering its size was the most powerful drug that they had given me so far. I was reluctant to take it but I knew if I didn't I would either have my visit stopped or would soon be dragged back in that room and subjected to people sat on my chest and water poured down my throat choking me. Therefore, I took it. Wow! it literally took less than ten minutes to take effect and I felt like I was having some sort of outer body experience like I had had in my lounge at home prior to being arrested.

Completely numb from head to toe I remained seated where I was just staring blankly at the wall in front of me. This drug was strong and completely did the job that it was set out to do as I wouldn't be telling my parents anything about the assault or about anything for that matter. The visit seemed to go by in a flash.

My mum and dad asked me questions but I was only able to occasionally nod my head or say the words "Don't worry I'm okay". I was far from okay but if that still meant protecting them then that's what I needed to do but, in all honesty, I wouldn't have been able to tell them the truth as that pill had literally erased any truth from my mind for the period of time that they were there. It's like someone had climbed into my brain with a wipe and dusted it over every little brain cell, erasing every bit of horror that I had endured the previous day. I just rambled nonsense (my memory of this is patchy, even now). I have since tried to find out what it was, they gave me, researching 'tiny blue pill' but as yet I have not been able to identify it. The visit didn't go as I wanted it to but was still comforting all the same. Just being in the same room as my mum and dad made me feel safe and secure which is something I missed dearly. The door opened and the female said that visiting time was up so we hugged, cried and said our goodbyes for another week. I stood at the window watching out onto the carpark and waved them goodbye until they got in the car and drove out of my view.

The medication was still taking effect but was starting to wear off slightly and the memories and horrors of yesterday had started to flood my mind again. If only I could pick up a phone and tell my parents to turn round and come back so that I could tell them all about it. The reality was I couldn't, they had made sure they had given me the right amount of medication to ensure that I wouldn't be telling any tales and I was guessing that the same would be happening next week. So, this was the end of week two now which meant I was half way and a step closer to getting out of here. However, two weeks of trauma and excessive restraint had only made my situation and paranoia worse and I felt I was in a worse place now than before I entered this place.

CHAPTER TWELVE

That night, the second Sunday in there has stuck in my head for reasons I wish I could forget. I went to bed as normal but was woken up in the middle of the night by rustling in my room. I thought I was dreaming at first but the longer it continued I realised that there was someone in my room. I slowly opened my eyes and sat up to find 'Scowl girl', my enemy sat in the corner of my room, the girl that had been giving me grief since I was brought in here. I didn't need to ask her what she was doing as I could clearly see that she was sat with her legs crossed making a Teepee out of sticks and then stuffing paper between them. In the other hand she had hold of a lighter and was flicking the lid up and down making a repetitive clicking sound. Was I dreaming or was this crazy girl really in my room preparing some kind of mini bonfire. I knew she didn't like me but apart from the glares and occasional shoulder nudge as we passed in the corridor, she had left me alone. I asked her what she was doing although it was obvious. She stated that 'Filth don't have a place in here and that I deserved to die and she would be the one to do it'. I couldn't believe what I was hearing. Not only did I have the staff against me and assaulting me but now I had physical death threats to contend to and potentially my room set on fire. I was meant to have been taken to a place of safety, somewhere where I would be protected. This couldn't be further from the truth; this place was hell and right at this moment I genuinely didn't think I would survive or ever see the outside of this building ever again.

She just sat there flicking the lid up and down and sparking the flame every now and again to make me realise that this threat or whatever her intention, was real. I sat there as still as I could as I didn't want to alarm her in any way. The longer the silence the more agitated she became and the more frequent the clicks of the lighter and longer she held the flame towards the pile of sticks and paper. I wasn't sure what her real intention was to be honest. In all honesty she had bluntly told me that she wanted me dead but I think I knew deep down that she was going to struggle to kill me with a small fire as my room was full of detectors including a smoke alarm directly above where she had set her stall out. I was also convinced that there was a CCTV camera concealed somewhere in my room so surely a member of staff must soon see what was happening and come and intervene. Whatever her intention she managed to put the fear of God in me and she knew it which I'm guessing was a good enough result for her, it meant she had power and control over the situation and me. It was a very strange period of time as we just sat there staring at each other. You're probably thinking why didn't I do a runner or shout for help! I contemplated this but what was the point. I would only be shouting for the bullies out there to come and save me from another bully in here and in all honesty, I didn't trust them to sort it or remove her. I tried my best to not come across as scared or intimated although it couldn't have been further from the truth as I was absolutely petrified. My decision though was the right one as eventually she got bored and gathered up all the twigs and paper, removing any evidence of her being there and left the room muttering a few words as she left, something along the lines that I should watch my back and that is what I intended to do.

I don't think I slept a wink that night, too terrified to fall asleep in case she came back to finish what she started. I just lay there waiting for it to become daylight. I always felt better during the day, if better is the right word, or at least that little bit less scared. Everything seems scarier at night and it sure did in this place as the building was even more dingy and eery. I told myself that it was now my third Monday which meant I only had this week and next week to get through and then I should be released. I had to find enough strength both physically and mentally to be able to get through and survive these next fourteen days. Don't get me wrong I know fourteen days doesn't sound like a long time but trust me, when you're living on adrenaline and fear, fourteen minutes seems like fourteen years let alone fourteen days.

I was told at breakfast that I would be able to go for an 'escorted' walk at some point this week if I caused no problems the days prior to it. How excited was I to have a bit of time outside, a bit too excited I guess but when you've been cooped up, no, in fact locked up for two weeks in such a horrific environment then the thought of even sticking my head outside the window seemed appealing. I played the game and nodded my head and thanked them. I actually thanked someone for letting me, an adult, a human being, a police officer go outside. It's ludicrous thinking about it now but at the time I would have gone along with anything as the first thing I thought and the only thing I thought was how I was going to plan my escape once I was let outside the front door.

Monday and Tuesday passed with nothing to really report. I stayed in my room for the majority of the time to try and avoid you know who. I knew I couldn't avoid her forever but I didn't want to go anywhere near her yet. I was too afraid of what the next threat might be and didn't want to be sleeping with one eye open. I needed all the sleep I could to build my strength up for the big escape. Wednesday soon arrived and I was told over breakfast that I could go for my thirty-minute escorted walk as promised. I was told to wait in my room and a member of staff would come and collect me when they were ready. I sat there patiently on the edge of my bed staring out of the cracks between the bars on my window. I remember it was a warm sunny day as I could feel the heat on my cheeks through the glass. The window was bolted down so I hadn't felt actual fresh air for two and a half weeks now and although I had been a hermit as such prior to being admitted I still loved the fresh air and being outdoors. So many thoughts went through my mind. Would I be handcuffed and have no chance to escape? If I wasn't handcuffed how many people would be with me, one on either side? If I managed to do a runner would there be high fences surrounding the perimeter? After all I had arrived very late two and a half weeks ago and it was pitch black so I had never had the opportunity to suss these things out. I basically had to risk assess these things once I was out there which was too much pressure on top of having the guts to actually do it, and try and escape. I had seen first-hand what they do to you when you don't follow 'their' rules and I was sure going to try my best not to find out what they would do if they caught me trying to escape.

CHAPTER THIRTEEN

Eventually a female member of staff appeared at my door and asked if I was ready. I nodded, stood up and followed her down the corridor towards the big all familiar metal door at the end. I half expected her to put handcuffs on me at this point, forgetting that I was actually at a hospital not a prison which was hard to do considering the treatment I had received. I've obviously never been to prison but by my reckoning they get better rehabilitation in there than I had so far. No handcuffs appeared and she opened the door and we both walked out into the next corridor and she shut the door behind us. The relief I felt as I heard that door shut and that horrendous corridor disappear before my eyes was indescribable. I followed her down the corridor passing the small room on my right that I was taken to on that first night and later taken to the floor and restrained, not knowing at the time that this would soon become a regular occurrence.

I had no idea where I was going from this point as I had not passed this point since, and the one and only time

I had I was in a world of my own and could have been anywhere that night. We walked down a small flight of concrete stairs, the handrail black and shiny like you get in a very old hospital or school. In fact, everything about this building was old, like something you'd see on a movie. Picture a mental asylum from the olden days and you wouldn't be far wrong. We arrived at the bottom of the stairs and came to yet another door, a larger door and I'm guessing the door to the outside world and fresh air. She unlocked it and pulled the door open and immediately I felt the sun hit my face in a flash. That feeling was the most uplifting feeling I had felt in such a long time. I felt like I could breathe properly for the first time since I was brought here. I was free to smell the air that actually smelt like air. I just stood there for a few seconds with my eyes shut taking it all in, the moment broken by the female telling me to get a move on as we only had thirty minutes. I stepped outside and remember having to wait for my eyes to adjust to the natural light and the glare from the sun. I'd only been used to artificial strip lighting and dark rooms so it took a few minutes for me to adapt. We walked across the gravel carpark and round the back of the dull prehistoric building to a large garden area scattered with benches in every corner, some taken up by other inmates on escorted leave. I only had about twenty-five minutes left now as five minutes had been taken up with actually getting there.

We walked round the perimeter of the grounds in silence at first and then the female started to make awkward polite conversation with me. To be fair to her there wasn't much for her to ask me given that I had been in here for the last couple of weeks and couldn't offer anything interesting to the conversation. She was probably too afraid to ask me anything personal in case it flipped me out in any way. Although I wasn't restrained it felt like it as she walked within an inch of my side, I'm guessing so she was able to grab hold of me quickly in case I decided to make a run for it which I had done nothing but think about since they told me this was happening and since I had stepped outside.

Every time we did a loop of the gardens, I scanned the area more and more looking for the best place to make my escape. I'm not going to lie it wasn't going to be easy as the majority of the grounds were surrounded in large overgrown bushes and tall trees which was probably done as a deterrent to make escaping a lot harder. However, I wasn't put off as I knew that this was my chance to get away from this hell hole and maybe my only chance so I had to try and formulate some sort of plan in my head. I hadn't got as far as figuring out where I would go if my escape was successful. That could wait as the most important bit was getting away and feeling safe and away from the bullies in this place. I was told that I only had ten more minutes and then we would have to go back to the ward. Right, this was it, I had to bite the bullet and go for it. I had already spotted a small clearance between a bush and a tree and could see the edge of an embankment. My only worry at the time was how steep the embankment was and where it led to. I couldn't over think it though as this seemed like the only possible place that I could run towards which gave any hope of my escape. I passed it one more time and decided the next time I reached it I would have to go for it as my time was nearly up. As we were approaching it, I started to gear myself up mentally for it. I could feel my palms getting sweaty and that all familiar sinking feeling in my stomach. As we approached it on my right, I tried to distract the member of staff by quickly pointing to something on her left in the distance and as soon as she turned her head, I was off in a flash. It may have seemed like a really weak plan but it was the only thing I could think of given how little time I had. No sooner had I darted off to my right that the female was right behind me shouting for assistance. She was able to catch me by grabbing hold of my top, however I had totally misjudged the embankment that I ran towards and before I knew it, I was tumbling down it at speed head first, hitting trees and branches on my way down.

I had not expected such a drop and to be honest when I finally came to a standstill, I wasn't sure whether I would be alive or not, let alone be able to pick myself up and keep on running. On the fall on the way down I guess you could say I was scared for a couple of reasons. One being that I would not survive it and two wondering what would happen to me next as there were bound to be consequences from this. After all I had seen and lived the punishment of not taking my medication and in my eyes, this was far worse and expected far worse punishment heading my way. Although I was scared for my life, I wasn't bothered what would happen to me and what injuries I sustained as I was thinking that if I was severely injured, I would have to go to hospital and would at least be away from this place for a while. No such luck though as when I hit the bottom, I was still conscious and still breathing and still able to feel my hands and feet. However, I had a very sore head from where I'd banged it numerous times. No sooner had I come to a stop that I could hear the shouting of staff and the rustling of leaves as they started to embark down the very steep muddy hill. I could hear one of them shouting not to move as the police had been informed and if I decided to carry on running, I would only be picked up by my colleagues and brought straight back. I distinctively remember this comment as it was said in such a sarcastic nasty tone, a comment that they wanted to remind me of my occupation but at the same time humiliate me. Trust me I was going nowhere; my plan had drastically failed and not only did I have to live with the failure and humiliation of my injuries I had to await my fate and see what my punishment was going to be.

Two of the staff got to the bottom and the look on their faces sent shivers down my spine. They didn't need to say anything as that look alone was enough to tell me that I was in a lot of trouble. They told me to get to my feet which I did with great difficulty but was determined to do it on my own as the alternative was having them scoop me up and I didn't want them anywhere near me.

The sting of cuts on my arms and forehead were starting to appear and I could feel the trickle of blood running down my face and as I went to wipe it away one of the men said "This is what happens when you do silly things". Silly things? I'm not five I thought, I'm a desperate woman on the edge who needed to get away from this place. Although I didn't regret trying to make a run for it, I felt like I could have done better. I probably should have used this first outing to suss things out properly and get my bearings. I was worried about doing this though in case I never got the opportunity again as outside visits were a privilege and had to be earnt, they weren't a given.

I was told to follow them, praying that I didn't have to climb back up that embankment. I was in so much pain and struggling to walk but I didn't want to show them and give them the satisfaction of preaching to me even more. Instead of leading me back up the embankment they took me round the bottom which led out onto a path back outside the dreaded hell hole. I half expected them to both grab hold of me but I suppose with the way I was walking and limping they knew I wouldn't get far even if I tried to run. One walked in front of me, the other behind and we were met by another four members of staff by the main door to the building. A little over the top I thought but what was new, they probably all wanted to be part of the drama. As I got to the door, I needed to decide quickly how I was going to behave. With the number of staff present I was under the impression that they thought

I was going to cause issues so I decided to do the opposite as I genuinely believed they liked people kicking off in these places, any excuse to show their authority and throw me to the ground. I reckon the majority of the staff had been bullied in their younger years and now they took it out on vulnerable, poorly people like myself, making them feel important and in charge. I'd dealt with people like this a lot at work and I could see through the majority of them and their ways. Don't get me wrong there was the odd 'okay' person in there but even they weren't the caring and supportive people that you would expect in these places.

CHAPTER FOURTEEN

All of them stood there staring at me waiting for me to do a runner and pounce on me or for me to kick off and pounce on me anyway. Instead, I lowered my head and walked past the army of staff guarding the main door, still slightly limping and in agony from all the cuts on my arms, and especially the one on my head. The staff filtered off behind me one by one and followed me along the corridor, back to the large metal door where the ward of doom awaited me. I started walking back to my room but someone took hold of my arm and led me back to the room where I had been restrained and forced tablets down my throat the week before. Once I was in the room, they left slamming the door behind them. Although I was back in that room all was too calm at the moment and it unnerved me. There was no way they were just going to put me in this room and that was it. There had to be some sort of punishment coming my way and I just sat there waiting for it. It came sooner than I thought as the door swung open and stood in the entrance was a large stocky male who I hadn't had the pleasure of meeting yet.

Behind him were numerous other members of staff, the majority of faces I recognised from different shifts. He was calm at first explaining to me that they didn't tolerate people trying to run off and that my behaviour was totally out of order. I nodded in agreeance so not to wind him up in any way. He then said that I was obviously agitated and that my medication wasn't working as I wasn't thinking or behaving rationally to have tried to run off. I tried to explain that I just wanted to go home but I could see that he wasn't interested in anything I had to say.

He then went on to explain that I was going to be given an injection to 'help me' and that it would relax me. I had no idea why they would be giving me this as I was completely calm since I had come back in the building and was in fact injured so why weren't they even offering to have my injuries looked at. They weren't interested at all in talking or even asking if I was okay. It was a case of I'd done wrong and I would now be punished and knocked out. I told him that I didn't want or need any medication and was okay which was obviously the wrong response as he started to move inside the room towards me followed by two members of staff behind him, one holding a very large needle. I started walking backwards, retreating away from them but the room was that small and pokey that I must have only gone three steps back before I hit the wall in the corner of the room. Next minute the staff pounced on me like a pack of wolves pulling me to the floor and restraining me. One of them pulled down my pants slightly on my leg and stuck the huge needle in the top of my thigh, whilst the others just stood there laughing and having banter between themselves. It all happened that quick that I didn't even have time to react let alone kick off with them. I'm not sure whether it was the same injection they gave me the first night but either way it was just as strong and started to take effect immediately. I felt every bit of life drain out of me and the conversation between them was just a mumble like I was under water and could only see their lips moving. I remember thinking that what they had just injected me with was totally unjustified as I had given them no cause to give me this. I had complied completely since being 'captured' at the bottom of the embankment and shown to be no threat. I thought that there would have to be some kind of grounds to treat a human being in this manner and everything would have to be documented, or would it. I still haven't seen my medical notes to this day so they could have written anything down to justify injecting me and knocking me out, but why? This is what I can't get my head around, even still to this day. Why treat me like a criminal and not a patient, a patient who had sustained injuries, all be it due to my own stupidity but never the less still injuries. Instead, they chose to knock me out. I think all they wanted to do was teach me a lesson, a lesson I wouldn't forget. Basically, if I ever tried anything like this again, not that I would probably be given the chance, or disobey any more rules then I would simply be knocked out!

Chapter Fourteen

I was knocked out good and proper as before I knew it the rest of the afternoon, and evening, had passed and I woke up to a new day. It was now Thursday. I spent the majority of that day in my room, still groggy from the injection they gave me the day before. I couldn't shift the banging headache and the heaviness in my arms and legs so decided to just lay on my bed and not fight it. I tried to move about but felt as though I was walking through treacle. After all there was nothing else to do and if I could keep a low profile for just over another week fingers crossed my release date would be here.

'Scowl Girl' had not reared her head again since the fire teepee incident in my room. Was she just having a bad day that day and decided to reflect her pain and frustration onto me or was she planning something else and I just hadn't been subject to it yet. Whichever it was I suppose all I could do was wait and see. Thursday went by in a blur, no one spoke to me other than to give me my meds or offer me food which I really wasn't interested in. No mention of my attempted escape yesterday or any welfare check on the cut on my head which by the way I had to tend to myself and still throbbed like mad.

CHAPTER FIFTEEN

Friday arrived and one of the staff came in my room early and told me that I had to make some effort to get out of my room and eat and even make the effort to get dressed and clean my teeth. It's really hard to get your mojo in places like this as not only has your self-esteem completely vanished by the time you get to these places but you don't see any point in having any pride about yourself as no one would appreciate it, let alone yourself. The female told me to brush my teeth and I told her I would when I was ready to. This didn't go down well as she then pushed me into my sink muttering under her breath "Do what you want then" It wasn't a particular forceful push or hurt me but it was enough to knock me off balance and stumble. I'm guessing it was another gentle reminder that they were in charge, not me, and if they told me to do something then I was to do it. The pushing and shoving happened more and more after that if I didn't do things straight away, that they asked me to do. This only sent me the opposite way as I didn't want to come across as a push over when I wasn't actually doing anything wrong. I've always been brought up to treat people with the respect they deserve and quite frankly not one member of staff deserved any of my respect in here.

It had nearly got to the end of week three and I still hadn't had any counselling or therapy of any kind, nor any one-to-one sessions with a key worker. I understand that when you're placed on a section 2, you're there to be monitored on your behaviour, and if by the end of the twenty-eight days you're safe to be let out back into the community. However, I was always under the impression that some sort of talking therapies would take place or meetings to help you aim towards a plan upon your release. I still hadn't received anything of the kind and there was no hint that it was to come in my so-called last week.

I only had the weekend to get through, which included one last visit from my parents on the Sunday, and then seven days from then. Surely, I could manage this, I had to if I stood any chance of getting out of here. So far, I had got in trouble for not taking my meds and trying to escape both of which were taken out of my hands now so basically there were no more rules to break, I could do this!

I was woken up Saturday morning to a loud disturbance coming from somewhere on the corridor, loud enough to make me want to get up and investigate. As I turned the corner onto the corridor, I could clearly see two police officers in uniform struggling with a large male. My instinct was to go and help as I had been in their position many times on wards like these. I knew I was living in cuckoo land though and left them to it watching them go back and forth with the male and stumbling with his weight. Eventually the staff came over and BAM, jabbed him straight in the bum enabling them to gain control and place the male in leg restraints. Why they hadn't done that initially is questionable. They then lifted the male and took him into the side room which was always left available for 136 patients, which meant they were brought in by the police to be assessed as they weren't deemed safe to be out in the community. One of the officers came out of the room to use his radio and I could hear him giving his colleagues an update, still slightly out of breath from the struggle. I saw this as my opportunity to try and engage with him. As I approached him, I asked if he was okay which came naturally as I always checked on my colleagues after a struggle, however he wasn't my colleague and looked me up and down like I was some nutter in this so-called nut house. I explained to him that I was a police officer and asked if he could pass a message on to my ex- partner for me. As I said her name his facial expression changed and must have thought for that split second that I was legit. I asked him to let her know that I needed her help and that I wasn't safe in this place. He nodded at me in a patronising way and gave me a half-hearted smile before being summoned back into the room. Who was I kidding. I was stood there in my PJ's, hair all over the place, dosed up to the eye balls, and as far as he was concerned, I was impersonating being an officer of the law. I didn't look like a decent member of society let alone a serving but non serving cop. There was no way that message would get back to her, no way at all. I had to try though and seeing that uniform again gave me sense of hope and the kick up the arse I needed to get my life back and wear that uniform again. The reality of it seemed a million miles away but I knew I had to try.

One more sleep to go I thought as I woke up that Saturday morning and I would get to see my parents. Hopefully for the last time in this place and then I would get to see them every day. A lot had happened since I saw them a week ago and I was determined to let them know all about it. However, my plan of this was soon stamped on as my 'key worker' (who I had only seen once in the last three weeks) said that he needed to have a chat with me that afternoon. My 'key worker' was an average built guy, name unknown, with short blonde hair. I can't really give any further description as one, I didn't really take much notice of him and two, he was bland so I didn't retain any description of him. I thought the meeting was going to take place in a side room on the ward but instead he came to my room, shutting the door behind him. He then sat on the end of my bed. I find it strange how I remember little things like this after all this time but I think I remember them for a reason. Although my key worker coming into my room and sitting on my bed might not seem like a major thing, it makes me feel emotional still to this day and I'm convinced more happened during that one to one that I have buried that deep into my mind that I can't remember or choose not to remember what happened. All I know is that when I think of it, it is vivid but scares the hell out of me. I've debated going for trauma counselling or something equivalent to see if I can unlock any memories about that particular incident but then what's the point. Who am I punishing other than myself. I would never be able to prove anything if anything did come to light and at the end of the day it would be a patient's word against a respectable member of staff and I'm guessing it's the latter one that they would believe. It doesn't keep me awake at night anymore thinking about it so I reckon its best it stays buried deep, at least for now. I don't want to spell out what I think might have happened but hopefully you are able to read between the lines and understand what I'm getting at. It would be wrong of me to make too much of an issue about this when I don't even know myself. However, it was yet another reality check that I needed to keep my mouth shut to my mum and dad and that is what I did.

CHAPTER SIXTEEN

Sunday arrived and I was told that my parents would be visiting before lunch. As predicted two members of staff came into my room half an hour before the planned visit, one of them holding a paper pot. They said "Now are we going to do this the easy way or hard way" pushing the pot in front of me revealing that little blue pill. The pill that I knew erased every bit of my short-term memory. I had two choices; one take it willingly and lose my memory or two be forced to take it and lose my memory anyway. It was an easy decision for me as I didn't want some staff member physically ramming their hand down my throat so I took it willingly. No sooner had I popped it into my mouth that that vegetative state hit my brain. Yep, I was totally numb again and could barely remember my name let alone tell my parents about my attempted escape, the staff forcing drugs down my throat and the key worker coming into my room which seemed a ridiculous tale to tell considering I couldn't remember a thing about it or whether I had imagined that part.

I was left alone for a while before being collected and escorted to my visit. As much as I was excited to see my parents I just wanted to lie on my bed and sleep the rest of the day and night. Hopefully though this would be the last time that they had to endure coming to this place to see their daughter locked up and that thought gave me the motivation to put a slight smile on my face as I entered the room. I think they were thinking the same thing as they seemed a little less stressed than usual and a bit more relaxed. Conversation seemed to flow slightly better than the last visit but my parents did most of the talking due to me being so out of it. They mainly talked about it hopefully being the last week in there and what plans they had for me once I was home. That four-letter word HOME filled my heart with contentment and safety. I still tried to remain optimistic though as I wasn't guaranteed to get out and anything could happen in a week. I nodded in all the right places and tried to show as much excitement as I could whilst being drugged up to my eyeballs.

My mum said that she had spoken to the ward manager on the telephone earlier in the week and they had told her that they were having some sort of case conference about me later next week and it would be then that they would decide whether I'm well enough, and safe enough, to be discharged from their care. The only saving grace was that my parents would be going and could fight to get me out. What a joke I thought! How can they use the word 'Care' in that sentence, none of the staff had shown one bit of care for me in the last three weeks. If anything, they had probably made my condition worse and messed my head up even more with the way they had treated me. Yes, arguably you could say they kept me 'safe' as in as much as I hadn't managed to do anything stupid to myself. However as far as psychologically, they had messed with my head beyond repair. I was paranoid when I entered this place and God knows what I would be like when I left as I didn't trust anyone anymore.

They chatted about the family and how my friends had been asking after me and couldn't wait to see me. I never understood why my friends had stood by me like they had as I gave them nothing back other than grief and worry. I'm glad they did though as the support that they showed me made me fight harder to get better. I'm in touch with the majority of those friends still today and I will forever be grateful to them. A couple of them distanced themselves from me when I started to get better and I appreciate and respect their reasons for this but again I will never forget what they did for me and how they supported me with visits in hospital to letters and cards of support.

As always, the visit was up very quickly and although it was upsetting saying good bye I thought that this could be the last time that I had to as the next time I saw them I would be leaving with them, hopefully! My dad gave me a hug and said he loved me which he rarely ever said. Not that I didn't have a strong bond with my dad, and I knew he loved me, but he was a man of few words sometimes, so those three words gave me that last bit of encouragement I needed to keep my head down and keep out of trouble for my last week. This seemed easier planned out in my head than in reality as I was totally put to the test during my last week which required every bit of strength I had both physically and mentally.

It started as soon as my parents left through the door. The member of staff that was guarding the door during my visit, as they always did, gave a snidey comment as I walked past her. She took hold of my arm ever so slightly but enough to stop me in my tracks and leant forward towards me whispering in my ear that she wasn't a fan of the filth and if she had her way, I would be going nowhere next week. I had never seen this member of staff before and, me being paranoid, automatically thought she was some sort of plant that had been put in here to kill me off so that I couldn't tell the truth to the outside world on how appalling people are treated in these places. I quickly gave my head a wobble and tried to rationalise it, it wasn't unusual to see new bank staff at the weekends and to be fair a lot of people hated the cops, even so-called professional people. It only took a couple of speeding fines to call yourself a cop hater. That's what I convinced myself anyway, it was either that or turn into a complete wreck for the rest of the week. Either way that comment made me want to spend the rest of my day confined to my room so I shut my door and tried to block out the shouting and screaming that was echoing the corridors on the other side. The only interaction I had for the rest of the day was to be given my meds.

CHAPTER SEVENTEEN

Monday was soon here and again I spent most of the morning in my room. Although I still had that sickly churning feeling in my stomach, I felt hungry as I hadn't eaten since breakfast the day before. As I entered the dining room, I felt like everyone was staring at me but in reality, they probably weren't, it was my paranoia kicking in again which had obviously been heightened since yesterday's comment. Nevertheless, I went to the food counter and made myself a couple of pieces of toast buttering it with the plastic knife that seemed to bend, bordering on snapping with every stroke. It seemed busier than usual and there weren't many empty seats other than the odd one scattered about between ram-packed tables. I wasn't in the mood to make any kind of conversation so opted for the spare seat on the quietest table by the window overlooking the gardens. The same gardens I had plummeted down the week before. No sooner had I sat down I felt a tap on my shoulder and when I looked up from my plate 'Scowl Girl' was stood over me. She appeared taller than I remembered but this was probably because I was sat down. She asked me whether it was true that it may be my last week in here as they were considering my discharge. I didn't know what to answer or what was the right answer in order to keep things easy for me but I was caught off guard and said Yes that's true. She smirked at me in a really chilling evil way and asked if I wanted her to make things fun for me before I left. I told her that I just wanted to keep my head down and didn't want any trouble but that seemed to fall on deaf ears as she just muttered something like "We'll see filth, don't want you leaving here without any memories". Any memories? Who was she kidding. I had enough bad memories to last me a lifetime. I didn't reply as I didn't want to fuel her so just looked away and back at my now cold floppy toast sitting on my plate. She lingered for a few seconds in an attempt to intimidate me a little more but I just focussed on my plate and was determined not to give her the satisfaction of looking up and letting her know that she had got to me. She eventually left and I felt like I could breathe again. I finished eating, if you call having a few bites of toasts eating and took myself off back to my room. I stayed there for the rest of the day, nervously waiting for something to happen whether it be from the staff or 'Scowl Girl'. Neither of these prospects were less scary than the other. However, I managed to get through the rest of the day without any incidents. Maybe if I kept my head down and stayed in my room for the next six days everything would go to plan and I would be released.

I was woken up Tuesday morning to a commotion going on in the corridor and when I peered out of my door, I could see the reflective strip of a police jacket rolling around on the floor trying to restrain a young male. Another day, another poor scared resident starting his sentence in this hell hole. I remember being one of those officers in these places like it was yesterday. I was so judgemental back then and didn't think twice about restraining someone without really thinking how it was affecting that person or how scared they would be. I promised myself that day that if I ever got to wear that uniform again, I would have more empathy for people in these situations and understand that they too have their own story and haven't got to this place for no reason. The reality of me ever being a police officer again seemed so out of reach but I guess I had to cling onto some hope as what would be the point otherwise.

Chapter Eighteen

My job still meant everything to me and even pretending to be a police officer again one day gave me that tiny glimmer of hope, the kind of hope I needed right now. They eventually managed to restrain the male and he was carted off to the 136 side room. I was about to go back inside my room when I caught a glimpse of the staff member that made that comment to me the day before. The sight of her sent shivers down my spine. She spotted me too as she started smirking and glaring at me as she walked down the corridor towards me holding a paper cup. No way was I taking any medication from her. She could have spiked it as after all she was a cop hater and I wasn't taking any chances. I quickly ducked back in my room but within seconds my door swung open and there she was, bold as brass holding the paper cup out in front of her. "Meds time" she said with that horrible smirk. I asked why she had suddenly appeared on the scene as she had not once given me any medication since I had been in here and after that comment the other day, I was convinced there was some plan being hatched. She said that I would be seeing a lot more of her this week and if I didn't want any problems then I should do as I was told and take my medication like a good girl. Patronising or what! A good girl? Yes, I wanted to keep my head down but I wasn't going to be a push over or let her get one over on me.

I looked inside the cup to see if the usual tablets were there and at a quick glance all seemed okay until I took a better look. I noticed that there was one bigger tablet that stood out, one that I had never seen or been given before. When you are given tablets on a daily basis, twice a day, sometimes three, you become very familiar with how many you take and the size, colour and shape of each one. Therefore, when I saw this one, I immediately knew it was new just from the colour and size of it. I challenged her about it but she was adamant that I had been taking this for weeks. Was I being paranoid and this was one of my usual drugs or was she just a very good liar. I decided to go with the latter and protect myself and took the pot from her hand and popped the tablets in my mouth one by one taking a sip of water after each one. She watched me intently, making sure that when I got to this 'suspicious one' I did actually swallow it. I popped it in my mouth, quickly shoving it to the side of my cheek and sipping some water. Her eyes narrowed as if to warn me that she knew I hadn't swallowed it. "Open your mouth" she shouted and as I slowly opened my mouth she stepped forward and grabbed hold of my arm and said if I didn't swallow it immediately, she would physically force it down my throat. Fear set in but I knew I had nothing to lose so told her I wasn't taking it till she told me what it was for, as I was a hundred per cent sure it was a new tablet. Given that my behaviour had not altered in the past few days and there was no sudden need for my medication to be altered, I was extremely convinced that there was some ulterior motive for giving it me. She refused to tell me and pushed me back on my bed forcing her knee on my chest in order to pin me down. She then attempted to force my mouth open with her fingers, in the meantime I spat the tablet out onto the bed. Her behaviour was definitely not that of a staff nurse, or any professional that should be working in this kind of place. I knew what they were capable of, as I had witnessed it first-hand but for her to singly act like this and not even raise the alarm to other staff which was protocol made me feel extremely vulnerable and for a split second I actually feared for my safety. I think at that moment in time she realised she had gone a step too far and quickly pressed her buzzer to get help which she should have done way before this. I reckon she just did this to cover her back. Within seconds I could hear the clatter of feet running down the corridor and before I knew it there were at least four other members of staff bursting through my bedroom door. The female informed them that I had refused to take my medication and become violent with her. I tried to explain my side of the story over the commotion that had erupted but I couldn't even hear myself think with the alarm and voices blaring in my ears so I guessed they couldn't hear a word I was saying. To be fair even if they could, they wouldn't have listened to a word I was saying. Why would they side with a patient over one of their own. They would have just taken it for granted that I had been violent and she needed assistance.

They all pounced on me from all angles, pinning my wrists down on the bed and their knees on my legs. I wriggled about out of fear not violence which only made them tighten their grip so decided to play dead and accept my fate. I knew I was either going to be jabbed in my thigh or physically have someone's fingers forced down my throat again in an attempt to get the tablet down me. Out of the two I decided that the jab would be the better option as at least I knew what to expect from the side effects whereas this tablet I had no idea. They however had the opposite idea and decided to try and ram the pill down my throat whilst another poured the water down. It brought back hideous memories of the other week and although this was on a slightly lesser scale it was still scary none the less. I fought and fought with every last bit of energy I had trying to lock my jaw shut in attempt to stop this unknown poison going down my throat and into my system. My strength paid off as they gave up a lot quicker than I anticipated and I recall one of them saying "Let's just jab her", whilst laughing, and yep, my pants were pulled slightly down and the needle plummeted into the top of my thigh near my buttock.

Chapter Eighteen

After a few seconds as predicted they each climbed off me as this stuff didn't take long to take effect and that all familiar paralysed feeling kicked in, yet again. As they left my room the female who was now clearly my enemy glanced behind me with a half worried look as if she had crossed the line in some way. I still don't know to this day what it was she was trying to give me or why but she had failed and funnily enough she never tried anything again. In fact, I never saw her again whilst I was in there. When I asked about her, I was told she was bank staff and only filled in for a couple of days. I muttered under my breath that they needed to do more extensive checks on the people they employed. I would never be able to prove it, like a lot of things that I encountered in this place over the weeks, but I honestly believe she was out to get me in some way. Whether part of this was my mind playing tricks on me, but the other part of me had a gut feeling about it and it felt very real.

CHAPTER NINETEEN

I'll skip forward now to Friday as the rest of the week was pretty much the same and luckily no incidents of note to write about. Just the usual boring day to day routine. Eat, sleep, meds, repeat! I thought the week was going too well until Friday came and 'Scowl Girl' reared her head. She had made it pretty clear to me in the dining room that morning that she was going to cause trouble for me before I went and that's exactly what she did that day.

It got to lunch time and I was in my room about to head off to the dining room for something to eat when she walked into my bedroom bold as brass with that cocky air about her. She stood there for a few seconds in silence with the intent of making me feel even more intimidated which I have to say worked. As she stared at me, I stared back at her short dark greasy hair that looked like it hadn't been washed in weeks, the dark puffy circles under her eyes like she hadn't slept for weeks. She was skin and bones like myself and every other person in here. Starving yourself and not eating was the last if not only bit of control you had over yourself so most people did it, plus the food was nothing to write home about, no Michelin star to say the least. Her clothes hung off her like they were three times too big for her, Nike T-shirt and jeans with rips in them and trainers that were once white but had now turned that really off white grubby colour. The silence was then broken when she said she had a small knife inside her jeans pocket, keeping her arm tucked into her side as if she was trying to conceal it. Still standing in silence we both just stood there staring at each other waiting for the first one to make a move of some sort. I was too shocked to speak and instinct told me that if I made a run for it or reacted in some way then she may panic and do something she hadn't even planned to do such as place that knife somewhere in my body. This was something I wasn't in a rush to find out so decided to try and use my negotiating skills that I had learnt in training, despite being a bit rusty of late.

I started by asking her why she had a problem with the police and in particular me as after all we were equal in here and I hadn't ever been otherwise out in the real world. She stood there moving her eyes to the side in a thinking mode mulling over the question before she replied. She took a deep sigh and went on to explain that she hated every 'cop' because of what they had done to her family. "Okay" I answered, trying to look as sympathetic and interested as I could at someone threatening me with a knife. I still wasn't convinced she had one as wasn't sure how she would have got one in here. The knives in the dining room were all plastic and other than getting someone to bring one in for her, it was almost impossible or was it. After all she had managed to get a lighter and threaten me with that previously, so nothing would surprise me. I'd seen how corrupt and evil the staff could be in here. Was it that cop hater staff that had threatened me. No, surely this was my paranoia setting in again. However, I aired on the side of caution and went with the pretence that she did have one, that way I wouldn't let my guard down and would be a bonus if she was bluffing.

I quickly answered "Why?" realising I had been distracted for a moment. She then went on to explain to me that she had been in and out of care all her life. The police raided her house when she was just five years old and arrested both her parents and hadn't seen them since. She said someone had planted a lot of drugs in their house to get them in trouble. Denial, a common trait for someone who knows the truth deep down but doesn't want to except it nor betray their parent's legacy.

Although she was stood there with the threat she had a knife, I almost felt sorry for her. How was she ever going to grow up to be a decent, law abiding individual when she had that kind of start in her early life. I surprised myself how calm and patient I remained, even though my heart felt like it was going to explode it was beating that fast. I realised that although I had been out of the police world for some time, you never really lose it. I told her that I understood why she may have this trust issue and hate for the police but that I wasn't out to cause her any issues, I was in fact poorly like her and was only in this place to get better. As soon as these words 'get better' came out of my mouth I thought what a load of rubbish and I'm sure she was thinking the same along with every other individual in this hell hole.

I could see that she was starting to get a bit more agitated, still with her hand in her pocket, I had an honest belief that there was a knife in there. She was starting to bounce a little on her feet from side to side which I had seen many times before in these situations. This was a common sign that they were getting more and more wound up and were about to either flip out or make a run for it. All of a sudden, she lunged forward and thrust out her arm in a stabbing motion with her fist clenched keeping the threatening arm still tucked down by her side. She shouted "Don't even pretend to try and understand filth, you have no idea what it's like to be me". No, I didn't, but she didn't know what it was like to be me either. Someone who had gone from a happy life and serving police officer to someone who gradually got severely mentally ill, attempted suicide and self-harmed and had every bit of their dignity and freedom stripped of them in an instance. Yes, my life had been good up until then unlike hers but believe me, my life had been turned upside down beyond recognition. I felt her pain to a certain extent but in a different way. I knew what it felt like to be let down by the authorities and in my case was the crisis team and NHS. Let down because I felt no one listened to me properly or offered me any therapy. Instead, they stuffed tablet after tablet down my throat till it fried my brain and sent me crashing. Anyway, back to 'Scowl girl', the female stood in my room threatening me with a knife that I still didn't know whether it existed or not. No sooner had she lunged forward, she had now stepped back muttering to herself. I knew I had to convince her to calm down but I hadn't worked out how exactly. Yes, I could have shouted for help but I knew that if I got the staffs attention she would get taken straight to segregation and pumped full of drugs. As much as I didn't like her and the way she intimidated and basically scared the life out of me, I knew how that felt and I wouldn't wish it on anyone, not even her. Plus, what was I going to gain other than an even angrier cop hater when she got out of segregation which was not appealing in the slightest. Who would have thought that my first instinct was protect her in some way after how she had been with me over the weeks. I think the penny finally dropped with her that I hadn't chosen to shout or run away and get her into trouble and this in turn this made her start to back off. I felt that we had somehow at that moment learnt some kind of strange mutual respect for each other. She slowly left my room and as she walked out of the door, she looked over her shoulder and gave me a slight smile as if to thank me for listening to her and not judging her. She was then gone and that is when I felt I could breathe again letting out the biggest sigh ever. I genuinely thought she was going to seriously hurt me when she first entered my room but turned out all she wanted was to vent and someone to listen. From that day she wasn't 'Scowl Girl' to me anymore as I no longer saw that, she was now 'Misunderstood girl'. Misunderstood in so many ways, a bit like myself, I guess.

CHAPTER TWENTY

It was later that day, on the Friday afternoon, that it was finally confirmed, I was finally leaving. A member of staff came to my room and told me that a meeting had been held earlier that morning by all the professionals that were responsible for me, including my parents. Long story short she said that there had been mixed feelings in the meeting over whether I should go home on Monday and that the only thing that swayed it was the fact that my parents had promised that they would take good care of me. My mum has since told me that herself and my dad had to attend numerous conferences about me. At one point, they weren't sure I would be allowed out. The doctors kept telling them that I was still too poorly to leave and ultimately, they could keep me in there a lot longer. My parents were completely against this idea as they could see the effects it was having on me being locked up in there. My mum recalls how thin I was at this time. She says I was literally skin and bones, she had to get me out of there fast if I was to survive this. My parents eventually managed to convince the psychiatrists and other 'professionals' that they could care for me at home and get me the help I needed. Thank God they did because they did in fact save me. I think if I lived alone or had no family to care for me, they would have left me in this place to rot. I feel sorry for all the people that are in this situation and are locked up in these places for months, even years on end. No wonder people get readmitted time and time again and, some, sadly take their own lives as they feel it is their only way out from the living torture, they endure day after day.

The relief at hearing these words was so intense the feeling was unbelievable. My nightmare would soon be over, or would it. Yes, the nightmare of being locked up in here twenty-four hours a day would be but, in reality, I was no better mentally than the day they brought me in, worse in fact. I still thought I was dying and now on top of that I had to deal with the trauma that I had gone through the last twenty-eight days and try and make sense of that. My fear now turned to how I was going to cope again in the real world. Would family and friends be under the impression I was fixed and back to old Beck? Would there be this expectation of me to get back to work straight away? So many questions going on in my head and no answers. I took a deep breath and decided that all I could do was take each day at a time. The main thing was I would be safe and no one could hurt me anymore or treat me like I was some nutter or just needed drugging up constantly. More importantly I would be able to go outside in the fresh air whenever I wanted and for as long as I wanted. Freedom, something that I had been deprived of for twenty-eight days. Even if I decided to stay in everyday it would be my choice, something else that I had missed.

Saturday was soon here and I kept thinking that this time tomorrow I will be able to say I can go home tomorrow. Best feeling in the world. The rest of the weekend went a lot better than I ever anticipated. No issues with 'Misunderstood girl' and that member of staff, was nowhere to be seen since that day she tried to drug me. I felt like things were going far too well but maybe my luck had finally changed and I was actually getting out of this place tomorrow. It's weird, because although I was still very poorly in myself, I slept like a baby that Sunday night. The thought of being at my family home, my childhood memories around me, my room, the night after, gave me a sense of calmness and safety.

I was woken up earlier than usual on the Monday morning as I needed to pack all my stuff up, albeit there wasn't a lot of my belongings I needed to get together. I had only been allowed the bare minimum from day one so it didn't take long for me to get a few clothes and my toothbrush together. All that was left for me to do now was wait for my parents to pick me up. I waited in my room until they arrived as I wasn't taking any chances for anything to go wrong and give them any reason for them to change their mind and keep me in hospital. I wasn't given a specific time of when they were coming and just told that it would be around lunch time as they had some discharge paperwork to sort out etc. The minutes felt like hours, the hours like days. As I was sat there, I reminisced about the last twenty-eight days and what I had gone through but most importantly survived. Although I was still ill and far from being better, I knew what faced me. I knew there was no quick fix and I knew I may never get fully back to my normal self but I was going to give it a bloody good try. I had to as not only did I want to get better, I felt I owed it to every single person who had helped me on this journey. I did worry though about whether I would suffer years down the line from what I had emotionally and physically endured whilst in here, but again I would have to deal with that as and when it happened. I only had the energy to focus on the present and that seemed impossible in itself. One thing I was certain of was that my ultimate aim was to get myself off any medication and as quick as I could. I totally blamed all this poison for landing me in here in the first place. I knew it wouldn't be imminent but I had to start it as soon as I could.

CHAPTER TWENTY-ONE

Finally, the time had come, twenty-eight days had passed and I got that final visit to my room. Not the usual visit to be given my meds or restrained in some way, but the visit to tell me that my parents were here and that I was going home. I couldn't take it in. Was someone going to come in and say it was all a joke or they had changed their mind. I stood up quickly and exited my bedroom for the last time as quick as I could before they had the chance to change their mind. I followed the member of staff down the corridor, noticing things as I passed. Silly things like people's initials etched on the walls that had probably always been there but I had been too preoccupied or drugged up to notice. The smell of disinfectant seemed stronger as well, one smell I would not forget. As we passed the communal lounge 'Misunderstood Girl' was sat on the chair facing the window and as I passed that exact spot our eyes met for the last time. We both gave a little nod to each other, no smile, just a sign of acknowledgment and to take care. Out of all my time in here, what started out as one of the scariest moments turned out to be one of my most memorable ones as it was the first time in a long time, I felt I gave someone that bit of empathy that they deserved.

I passed the nurses office with the large clock above it which read 1.30pm and the all-familiar radiator opposite where I spent many an hour, sat staring out of the large window. I was then led to the meeting room where my parents were waiting. There were no words and none needed at least for the time being. We were all content with just hugging each other and seeing the stress and anxiety lift off us one by one. The member of staff told us to sit tight as they were just finishing off the discharge papers and sorting out all my medication to take home. It's like I had gone back into child mode as I sat on my mum's knee with part of me still thinking that it wasn't guaranteed that I would be going. I wouldn't actually believe it till I was out of the doors and sat in the back of their car.

The ward manager for that day entered the room holding a big paper bag in one hand, containing my cocktail of drugs and paperwork in the other. She did a quick run through of what I needed to take, how many and when, explaining that everything was written on the packets if we needed reminding. She then asked my dad to sign a piece of paper explaining that he was signing to confirm that I was being discharged into their care. We were also given a list of contact numbers, should I need them, which included the Crisis Team which I wouldn't be calling in a hurry.

"Okay you're free to go" she finally said wishing me good luck as I left through the big metal doors. I only had the corridor and a flight of stairs to walk down and I would be free. We followed a member of staff, the jingling of keys hanging off his belt echoing in the corridor. I couldn't help but look over my shoulder at every opportunity as I was convinced someone would follow us. My paranoia was the highest it had been for a while and I just couldn't shake off that feeling of being followed.

We walked down the flight of concrete stairs and reached the large main door, the last time being here was when I was escorted back from my attempted escape. The door swung open slowly and the fresh air hit me instantly. I followed my mum and dad out into the courtyard and the door shut behind us. I really was getting out! My dad took hold of the small bag I was carrying and we walked towards their car parked in the corner of the car park. I climbed in the back, my mum and dad in the front and the engine was soon started. My mum reached her hand out to me in the back seat and squeezed my knee telling me that everything was going to be Okay from now on. The fifty-minute journey home seemed to take forever and I was constantly looking out of the back window to see if we were being followed. I remember telling my dad to drive faster and get us home as there were people behind us and would know where we lived. I couldn't get my head around just being let out and being able to tell people how I was treated in there. I genuinely believed that I would be watched for a while so not to break my silence of the horrific things I was subjected to. I'm guessing though that this was just my mind playing tricks on me, my psychosis rearing its head again. They probably just banked on no one believing the drugged-up nutter if I was to ever disclose what happened.

Chapter Twenty-Two

We arrived home and although I felt a sense of relief, I still had that churning feeling in my stomach and the constant worry. I felt deflated, as all I wanted was to be coming home and be better. When you go into hospital for an operation and get picked up, you're usually fixed and can't wait for the comfort of your own home to continue with the recovery. However, this was so different. With a mental illness, more often than not you get released from these places no better than when you went in, worse in some circumstances, just like mine. This is hard for people to accept and understand as you can't see a broken brain. So, although I felt happy to be home, I wasn't happy if that makes sense as I just wanted to be normal but was far from it. My parents had gone to so much effort to make things nice for me but all I wanted to do was go to my room and be alone. I know that may sound ungrateful but I wasn't used to making conversation or being around people so I felt a bit overwhelmed by everything. My parents were so understanding though and left me to it. I think they were just content with having me back under their roof.

Late that night my mum brought the bag of medication up to my room, not in a paper pot thank God. We went through what I needed to take and she sat with me whilst I took them. I didn't blame her for not trusting me to take them alone as I had betrayed them in the past with this and I had to earn that trust again. I briefly mentioned to my mum that I wanted to start reducing my meds and get my brain back to normal. She agreed with this but said we needed to do it the right way and that she would speak to the doctor about it. As I fell to sleep that night, I tried to convince myself that tomorrow would be a better day as I was in a safer place and it would be the start of my recovery. However, I woke up early that next day and as soon as I opened my eyes realisation hit me that absolutely nothing had changed and I was still trapped in this living nightmare. Yes, I was in a familiar, safer environment but I was still stuck in my head with the thought of death being imminent. I suppose I was naïve to think that I would be fixed overnight. I remember getting out of bed and pulling back the curtains and just watching the neighbours getting in their cars to go to work and carry on with their normal routine. Something as simple as this made me explode with jealously. I wanted to be them, I wanted a normal boring everyday routine again.

It's so hard to explain that feeling that you get when you don't feel like you anymore. It's not just a feeling of sadness, otherwise labelled as depression, it's more than that. It's like you've died inside and you don't see any way of getting better no matter how hard you try. That is why I did those silly things to myself which ultimately got me locked up. I would be lying if I hadn't thought things since. Again, not because I wanted to check out, but because I no longer wanted to feel this drowning sensation anymore. I always thought suicide was selfish but I understand it now and I genuinely believe that the majority of people that take their own life don't want to die. They too just can't cope anymore with that feeling, the feeling of desperation and not knowing how to claw back their own life back, and unless you've been through it yourself, you'll never understand or come close to understanding how it feels. To truly understand mental health, I genuinely believe you have to have gone through it yourself. If you break your leg, people can sympathise and even understand the pain you're going through even if they've never broken anything before. It's so different with your brain though as people can't climb into that and observe what's happening in there or even begin to understand how it's effecting you. That is no one's fault or ignorance, it's just how it is.

The next few days were pretty much the same. I literally just lay on my bed staring at the ceiling only going downstairs to eat my meals. I felt so bad on my parents but I think they understood I just needed a bit of time. Before I knew it, those awful thoughts that I was dying were getting stronger and I felt that no one could help me. My parents tried to convince me that I wasn't but no matter what they said I just didn't believe it. Every little bump and lump I felt in my body, I was convinced was a sign that I was terminally ill. It's absolutely crazy to think of it now but at the time it felt so real. Why had these thoughts suddenly got so strong and frequent again. The only thing that calmed me down was a visit to the doctor's surgery which became the only place I left the house for. I was literally there with every mark I could find on my body and although they did their best to convince me that it was nothing to worry about, I soon found something else to go back with. It became a vicious circle and once again I became completely obsessed with it. The only conversation I had with my parents was about me dying and how the NHS knew but were covering it up as they didn't want me to survive. I bet reading this makes you realise just how poorly I was again and how much I had lost the plot. The reality was I was suffering from yet another psychotic breakdown and I needed help fast.

CHAPTER TWENTY-THREE

My poor parents probably thought I'd start to get better once I was home and my brain would start to heal. However, nothing had changed really. I had had no talking therapies whilst in hospital as I wasn't offered them. I was still drugged up to the eyeballs and I had no idea what the cocktail of drugs was doing to my brain. Although my mum and I had discussed decreasing the medication the doctor wasn't happy to just yet as they wanted to give it a bit of time for me to adjust being out of hospital. However, I was spiralling again and the suicidal thoughts had returned and there I was yet again running across the fields opposite the house late at night with my dressing gown cord. I couldn't believe it was happening again and I was doing this to my family once more. The fact was I couldn't help it, it was out of my control. That switch had just gone in my head again. My mum promised me that they would keep me safe and not allow anyone to lock me up again and I begged her to keep this promise as I didn't think I'd survive a second time in there.

Doctors eventually reviewed my medication again and I was moved to a different anti-psychotic drug which took a while to kick in and, in the process, made me pile the weight on. I literally went from a size eight to a size sixteen in a few months. The heaviest and most unattractive I had ever been in my entire life. This then affected my self-esteem and confidence even more, which I didn't think it could get any lower. The thoughts never stopped and I acted on them a couple of more times, taking a pathetic number of tablets, probably five more than the 'safe limit'. I knew this wouldn't kill me but got the unwanted attention I had been trying to avoid the last few weeks.

I ended up at A&E and because it had been a deliberate amount taken it was protocol to see the crisis team before I could get discharged. How could I be so stupid to allow myself back in this situation and potentially get myself chucked back in hospital. That's just the point though, I wasn't thinking straight or rationally when I took the tablets, I couldn't have been to even have slightly risked this. That's what happens when you suffer from psychosis. All your instincts and rational thinking goes out of the window and you can't, and don't, think of the consequences before it's too late. Long story short I saw the crisis team who were already up to speed on my past having read my file before seeing me, thank God, as I really didn't have the energy or inclination to relive everything. They asked the usual tick box questions, how is your mood at the moment? Do you have feelings of self -harm? They then left the room to discuss the best way forward. It wasn't long before they reappeared round the cubicle curtain. They asked me once more to explain why I had taken the tablets. I had to think quickly here as my fate, going forward, depended on what I said. I explained that I had been struggling since being discharged from hospital, a few weeks earlier, and that I didn't want to die and had merely had a relapse and that what I did was a cry for help more than anything else. I think I convinced myself just as much as them and although the majority of what I was saying was the truth part of me felt disappointed that I couldn't be completely honest with them. Honest in that I just wanted the drowning feeling to disappear and for my brain to stop. I knew though that I couldn't say this as it would give them that flickering of doubt as to whether I was a danger to myself which meant they had to lock me up again for my own safety.

My mum was amazing as per usual and promised them that I would never be left alone and that we would get a plan together with the crisis team who were scheduled to visit the house the next day. This was the first visit, must I add, since I got home, other than the odd telephone call to check in and see how I was doing. I know these people are busy and run off their feet as I'd witnessed it first hand at work, but come on, how are you ever meant to get a true reading of how someone is coping over the phone with a quick five-minute chat. This was just another hole in the system and how I was let down and as much as I didn't want to see them, I had to go along with it for now.

We drove back home from the hospital in silence. I couldn't look at my mum's face as the pain and shock on it made me feel worse and so guilty. The only time I spoke was to reassure her that I would make more effort. Even if she didn't believe this it made me feel slightly better at the time.

CHAPTER TWENTY-FOUR

There was a knock at the door and I knew I had to haul myself out of bed and make myself look half decent as I heard my mum greet the crisis team at the front door. I shouted that I would be down in a minute. I gave myself a quick pep talk in the mirror in the bathroom and promised myself that I would be pleasant with them, well as pleasant as I could be with these people. I entered the lounge to find a man and woman sat on the couch, relief that it wasn't the two women that had me removed from my home months earlier. We talked briefly about my time in hospital and as much as I wanted to expose the truth and how these places should be shut down, I didn't. I would tell someone one day but now wasn't the right time. I had to be fully better before I told my story if I was to be given any chance of people believing me. We then discussed the tablet situation. I said the same again, that it was a cry for help and that I had started to decline the last week and think scary things again. I was taking a gamble here as I was being a lot more honest than I was going to be. The more honest you are the more

118

chance you'll get carted off. I was willing to take the chance though as I wanted to get better more than anything and I knew that if I didn't do something drastic, I would just be stuck on this hamster wheel going round and round not getting any better. I didn't want this to be my life, I wanted to get my life back.

So, I just blurted it out that I thought I needed to go somewhere as a voluntary patient to give my brain a bit of a rest and to completely review my medication under the supervision of professionals. I stipulated straight away that I would not entertain going back to that hell hole and that it had to be somewhere local to my mum and dad so they could visit on a daily basis. I needed that regular contact to keep me focussed on my recovery and to feel safe. My mum squeezed my hand and gave me that look of pride, the same look she had given me on the day of my passing out parade from the police. We had discussed things the night before and how I needed to do something drastic before it was too late. I think she thought I would bottle it and to be fair I very nearly did as the thought of going back into any type of hospital like this terrified me. However, it was different this time as it was my choice, and I hadn't been physically forced to go and I knew I could leave when I wanted. This was the first positive step to my recovery and it felt good. I had a long way to go, but I felt like I was finally moving forward instead of backwards.

The crisis team made a couple of calls to see what beds were available and where, and within half an hour got a call back to say there was one available the next day at a hospital only ten minutes away from my parent's house. I confirmed that this would be okay. Don't get me wrong it was far from okay as I really didn't want to go but I had to. I had to do this for myself and for my family. I didn't sleep well that night with the torment of whether I had made the right decision. I was scared that some of the staff from the first place might now be working there and have it in for me. The chances of this were slim but the thoughts were there none the less. I must have eventually drifted off to sleep, probably from the exhaustion of over thinking and worry.

The day arrived and my parents dropped me off at my new home for the next seven days. It felt different this time. Just being dropped off instead of carted off, it felt calmer, I felt calmer. It wasn't too dissimilar to my last place as I was met at the door by a member of staff and my parents had to say their goodbyes. At least I would see them the next day and the day after that.

The doors shut and I waved them goodbye through the glass panel. I didn't think for one minute I'd be back on a ward so soon, if ever. I walked down the corridor which was a lot shorter than the last place and shown to a large communal room. I think when people design these place's they tick the box 'make the place look as drab as possible' and that it was, drab! The same old plain walls and fake leather settees with the odd picture hung on the walls that staff have probably brought in rather than throwing out during a clear out in their attic.

Chapter Twenty-Four

I was shown to a table where a female was sat waiting for me. She was introduced as my key worker which was a surprise as I had only just got in there. I was in that hell hole for twenty-eight days and not introduced to a soul, other than that episode in my room that one time. I remember she was kind and appeared like she genuinely wanted to help me. We spoke about my medication but in a positive way as I had made it very clear prior to coming in here that this was one, if not the main thing I wanted to get sorted and fast. I wanted to decrease my dosage as much as I could so I felt in the real world again but not too much so that I had some sort of relapse. Although I didn't trust many people, I had to let my guard down ever so slightly and trust that they were listening to me and would help me, so I decided to trust my key worker.

After I had finished with her, I was shown to my bedroom, again a number of differences with this as well from the last place. First thing I noticed that there were no bars on my window which in turn made the room feel warmer and brighter, and somewhat cosier. There was a desk with drawers and a small table lamp in the corner and my bed opposite which looked like a proper bed, one you would find in a house. Not a hospital type bed with plastic sheets on. Although I was still apprehensive about it all I felt slightly more relaxed. I guess the fact I walked in here, rather than being dragged in and jabbed with a needle which knocked me out, made it all a more pleasant introduction. I was given a sheet with my meal times and another sheet with daily recreational activities that took place. Don't get me wrong it wasn't like the normal gym timetable I was used to but at least it was something, something to try and keep myself and every other person in here sane and active.

I stayed in my room for a while, updating my diary which I had tried to do every day since this nightmare began, and this is the reason, I have been able to write this book today. I wouldn't have remembered all this had I not at least made some notes, no matter how little, as they were something to jog my memory. The bell went for tea time so I headed off to the dining room which was pretty much full by the time I got there. I spied a seat on the way in and headed for that which was good as it was the smallest of tables and had fewer people to make conversation with, something that I no longer liked doing anymore. There was still the odd poorly person knocking about as not everyone like me had come in here voluntarily and some were on a section. Even those on a section were luckier than I had been as I would much rather have been brought here first time round from what I had witnessed so far.

I made polite conversation with a few of them, nothing major, just exchange of names, age and why I was here. I was happy to give out the first two but not happy to share my story with anyone just yet. It would take a lot of trust to open up to anyone about that. A couple of them were happy to tell me all about their life, too much really but

I sat there regardless and listened in silence as I felt they just needed to get things off their chest. I've learnt how to do this over the years and very rarely keep things bottled up anymore.

I finished eating and glanced at the clock, 6pm! Only half an hour to wait until this evening's activity which was pool. I used to love pool, especially as a kid. Although I didn't have much enthusiasm for anything I made myself go. I had come into this place to get better which I couldn't just sort by tweaking my meds, I needed to push myself a bit more. I know going along to play a game of pool probably doesn't seem much but trust me at the time it was. I had lost all my confidence in everything which included social interaction with people. Something that had always been so easy for me now seemed like a major task. This was the start though to my recovery and I was determined to try, even if it was baby steps to start off with.

I got to the pool room which was off the corridor I had walked down when I arrived. As I entered it there were a couple of people already playing a game and greeted me with an 'Hello' as I walked through the door. I muttered hello back as I hung my head down, too shy and socially inept to look at anyone. I plonked myself down on one of the chairs in the corner and watched the game. There was a lot of laughing going on which was nice to hear as I had only heard screams the time before. I was soon asked if I wanted a game and forced myself to say yes. I'm not going to get ahead of myself and say I enjoyed playing but when it was finished and I was back in my room I felt a sense of positivity for the first time in a long time. I can honestly say I was proud of myself for stepping out of my comfort zone.

CHAPTER TWENTY-FIVE

There was a knock at my door followed by a voice saying it was med's time. I opened the door and let them in. I immediately saw the white paper cup in their hand which sent shivers down my spine and right back to my time in that hell hole where I was subjected to all that trauma. They popped it down on my desk and then left the room. No thrusting the cup into my hand or standing over me to make sure I took them. They had actually trusted me to take them. After all I had asked to come in here for some help so if I couldn't be trusted to do this then there was no chance of any recovery, and the fact they gave me a bit of independence and trust made me all the more determined to take them and follow the rules.

That is what I did for the next six days, I followed the rules to the letter. I went to every meal time and actually ate as I knew I needed to build my strength up again, took my meds when asked and attended every activity that was on offer getting more and more confident by the day. I think it helped because my family and even my auntie came to visit on a regular basis who I was always very close to. I was still scared at night when everywhere went dark and there was no noise to distract me. Scared that a new member of staff may come on the ward and have it in for me or a new patient being admitted that found out I was a cop and made my life hell. However, this never happened and before I knew it, I had done my seven days. During this time my medication had been completely reviewed and although I was kept on some of the same things, I was also taken off some and I had already started to feel the benefit of as my head didn't feel as fuzzy and I could actually hold down some sort of conversation. The gamble of going in there paid off as I could now see light at the end of the tunnel and every day was an up-hill climb, not a slippery slope.

I haven't talked about my time in here in as much detail as I could. I merely wanted to highlight that to start the recovery after such a traumatic experience, you have to tackle it head on, and sometimes you may have set backs along the way. I never thought, for a second, that I would voluntarily go into a similar place to the one that had messed my head up so much in the first place, but I knew I had to do something drastic as I was heading back to a very dark place. It paid off though as that week not only gave me the confidence but the understanding to go forward in my recovery. I knew now that I wasn't too far gone to be one of those unlucky people that would spend the rest of their life in and out of various hospitals around the country. I had proved to myself that I still had enough fight in me to beat this and get my life back. It also opened my eyes that not all psychiatric hospitals are the same and like every profession and work place there are good and bad people and places. This time I had dropped lucky thank God.

CHAPTER TWENTY-SIX

My parents picked me up and I think they could see immediately that I had improved slightly. I walked towards them rather than shuffled and I held my head high rather than looking to the ground in shame. I wanted them to see that I was serious this time in getting better and the way they smiled at me when they saw me gave me even more strength.

Life resumed as normal, well the new normal for the next few months. There were up and downs as expected and I still spent the majority of time in bed hiding away from the world. There were times when I thought that week's stay had been a waste of time as I seemed no better really and had just slipped back into a non–existent life again. My friends wanted to come and see me and as much as I wanted to let them, I still didn't want people to see me this way so kept putting them off. My sister kept in regular contact with me as she was still living in America. She offered to pay for private counselling for me and although I wasn't in the mood to talk to anyone let alone a stranger,

I decided to give it a go. It seemed ungrateful to turn it down plus I had nothing to lose I suppose.

My mum dropped me off at the building out in the sticks and I sat there for one and half hours, the first twenty minutes were introductions and what you call an ice breaker to make me feel more comfortable. I knew how it worked as I had had counselling before but for different reasons whilst in the Police.

The first time I was referred for counselling was after I had attended a murder of a sixteen-year old boy, which I later learnt was a dispute over a girl. It was very early on in my career and I was first on scene. It was like something out of a horror movie and at twenty-two years of age I had only ever seen things like this on the TV. The boy had been stabbed through the heart once, in his own home, by known associates who had fled the scene by the time I got there. He was lying on the lounge floor in a blood bath, barely breathing. I had completed many courses early on in my career, in particular first aid training for these situations so knew I had to act fast. I was still the only officer on the scene, and with the family hysterical around me, I started CPR on the boy. I can still hear the screams from the family today. There is nothing more distressing than the screams of a mother watching their son slip away in front of them, it's chilling. I carried on for what seemed like an eternity but was probably five minutes at the most before the ambulance arrived on scene. Prior to them getting there the boy murmured something to me which I found hard to understand at first through the gurgling of blood in his mouth but realised he had said "Don't let me die". No sooner had he said this his head slumped to the side and it was at this point that I knew he was gone. I had to carry on with CPR though, for the family's sake and in these cases young people are worked on a lot longer as they can be revived. The paramedics took over and I stepped back, my uniform covered in blood and my mind spinning from what I had just had to do.

The paramedics worked fast and once they had stabilised him or should I say looked like they had stabilised him they carried him out on a stretcher to the back of the ambulance. My colleagues had arrived by this point and I was asked to drive the ambulance to the nearest hospital so the two paramedics could carry on working on him. We were only about a ten-minute ride away from the hospital, five minutes the speed I drove, in fact I don't remember that journey in the slightest. Adrenalin completely took over and all I could think was if I could have done something differently to save him. I was already blaming myself for being inexperienced and should someone else have been first on scene, with more experience, he could be alive in the back, albeit very poorly, but alive.

We arrived at hospital and things moved so fast. I knew this was a murder so I had to stay with him at all times for continuity before the circus arrived. We went straight into resus and I literally had to watch this poor boy's chest be ripped apart so they could start massaging his heart. I genuinely felt like I was having some sort of outer body experience. Everyone expects that because you're wearing that uniform that you're immune to any emotion. I was a twenty-two year old, fresh out of training, only ever having seen anything slightly similar to this on Casualty on TV on a Saturday night. Never in a million years when I started my night shift that night at 10pm, did I think I would I be stood here now having just had a sixteen year old boy die on me and be covered in his blood watching all these people trying to bring him back from the dead. I was literally shaking like a scared little girl and that's exactly how I felt, scared!

My police radio was blaring away asking for updates and as scared as I was, I calmly updated them of the situation and that I would have to go into radio silence whilst I was in the resus room. It wasn't long after that that my supervisor entered the room, God I was glad to see him. Before I had chance to brief him on anything I remember hearing the consultant say to everyone "TIME OF DEATH......" It was official, he was gone. Bigger bosses had arrived at this point and CSI (Crime Scene Investigator), and I was told that all my blood-stained uniform would have to be seized for evidence. The boy got put back together, in as dignified a way as possible, and he was then moved to a side room so CSI could start their work. Again, for continuity I had to follow them and sit there whilst this poor boy's body was poked at for evidence. Every swab, nail clipping and hair clipping I had to endure whilst still sat in my wet uniform, wet from the fresh blood that had now seeped through to my skin. The main thing that has always stuck in my head about this part of the job was when the CSI officer put a plastic evidence bag over the boy's head, both hands, and both feet, tying them with a cable tie. That image has never gone. I understand why they did it, to preserve evidence, but I wish I hadn't had to see it. When the officer was done, she then handed me a paper suit and trainers and asked me to individually place each piece of my uniform in the bags laid out on the table next to the stretcher the boy was lying on. I wasn't bothered I had to strip in front of two people, well one that was aware of my presence. I just wanted it off as quickly as possible. Big bosses were still coming and going and I had to repeat my story at least three times before they finally left me alone. All this took hours and it was now in the early hours of the morning when I should have been winding down after my night shift but in reality, I still had lots to do with little brain function left. CSI packed up and advised me that the victim was okay to be taken to the mortuary whilst covering him over with a white blanket. These days, in the police world, a porter would do this accompanied by a police officer but that night, it was my job which I had to do alone because of it being in the early hours, and the fact that everyone else was running around trying to catch the scum that had killed him.

The mortuary was just across the car park from the hospital, a small ugly grey building. I wheeled him out of the side room and out of the back doors of resus into the dusk cold air dressed in my paper suit like I had just been released from custody. I had been given a swipe card for the door and as I entered the lights came on, thank God, as these weren't nice places to go into, let alone at that time of the night, and on your own. That mortuary smell hit me instantly which can only be described as cleaning products and death. Something you will only recognise if you have the unfortunate experience of smelling first hand. I checked the book for a spare place in the fridge and luckily there was one at the bottom which made it so much easier for me. I placed him in as carefully and respectfully as I could, filled out his details in the book and made a dash for it, slamming the main door behind me.

This would never happen in policing today as welfare is highlighted and recognised a lot more especially after jobs like this. Like I said you would never be expected to go to the mortuary on your own either like I did but back then that's how it happened. When I finally got home late that morning, I did get a quick welfare check from the boss over the phone. When he asked me if I was alright, I had to literally bite my lip to stop myself from crying. I was new and felt I had to act as though I was alright, not that I was a complete an utter mess and contemplating already whether I was cut out to be a police officer.

Before I knew it, I was back in the room, sat there in front of my counsellor having run through this whole incident, in absolute tears, unaware of how much this job still affected me. I had only been in there over half an hour and I had opened up to this complete stranger. This led us on to talking about all the other horrific deaths I had dealt with in the six years of my career so far. I thought I was there to talk about my breakdown, not all this but it makes sense now as she was trying to figure out why I had gone from living a normal life to having a major psychotic breakdown and why so quickly. The time went so fast but we ended the session on an incident where I had found a young male hanging from underneath the pier, again early on in my career and the first hanging I had been to. The counsellor told me to have a think over the next week about how this had affected me and we would pick it up next week. Prior to entering this room, I had it in my head that this would be a one off and I would not be returning. I had a different perspective on it now though as it felt quite good to speak about everything and to have someone listen to me without judging me.

I left the room thanking her, but in a daze, and completely emotionally drained. I drove back in silence with my mum, she didn't ask me anything as she could clearly see I had been crying from my puffy red eyes. I updated my diary when I got home but didn't go into detail about the incidents we'd spoken about as they were etched on my brain and always would be, I thought.

CHAPTER TWENTY-SEVEN

That week my mum got a phone call from work saying that two of the bosses from my department wanted to come and visit and have a chat with me about the way forward and my future within the police. I suddenly got nervous as I had blocked out work recently as I wanted to focus on my recovery. I also made myself believe that I would still be a cop again one day and I didn't want anyone coming to my home and shattering that dream, not yet anyway. This was one of the main things that kept me going and had been throughout all this. I had adored my job once and I would adore it again. I understood though that it needed to be done so told my mum to let them know I was ready for that visit anytime.

I never thought that 'anytime' would mean the next day but here we were sat in the lounge at my parent's house with the two big bosses of the Senior Management Team (SMT) of the Public Protection Unit. They did the pleasantries of asking how I was but I could see that they weren't that bothered really and when I answered their questions, they had their heads down taking notes and getting ready for the next question before digesting the answer from the last one or even absorbing what I had said. One of them got straight to the point and told me that if I was to return to work, I would not have my position on the Public Protection Unit anymore. I kind of understood as I had been through a major breakdown and this department deals with the most vulnerable of society so I guess they would be taking a risk placing me back on there. I would have been fine with that but his comment didn't just stop there. He went on to say that as long as he was in charge of the Public Protection Unit, I would never be allowed back on there even in years to come if I had fully recovered. Kick a horse while they're down sprung to mind. It was the way he said it as well, so abrupt and matter of fact. It was as though he was trying to punish me in some way for having been mentally ill, something I hadn't chosen. Even if he felt like that, he didn't have to say it, as it left me feeling like a complete nutter and totally deflated again. I couldn't hide the fact that he had upset me and had also got my dad's back up.

My dad told him that he didn't appreciate him coming into our home and speaking to me in this manner when all I needed was support and kindly asked them to leave. I was relieved as I could feel my anxiety levels going through the roof and I was worried I was going to say something I would regret as they were still my bosses at this time. I also didn't want to give them any ammunition that I was still that mad girl that got physically removed from her own home by her colleague's months before. I wanted to prove to them and come across like I was recovering, which I was but very slowly. As they left, they told us that someone would be in touch about a welfare meeting. Whatever, I thought, I'd already lost my dream job, the job I'd worked so hard for, so what could they do to me now. To be honest, at that moment in time, I wasn't even bothered.

CHAPTER TWENTY-EIGHT

My counselling soon came round again and we picked up where last week's session had finished about the job involving the hanging. She had asked me to have a think about that particular incident but I couldn't really think of anything to say other than how it made me feel finding someone like that. I knew what she was getting at as she would obviously have access to my notes and the suicide attempts that I had done with the dressing gown cords. I know I hadn't actually made a serious attempt but she probably wanted to see if it was linked in any way. Personally, I don't think it was as it was over six years since I had witnessed my first death by hanging and I had seen so many more since. Yes, they weren't pleasant but I had been to other jobs that had affected me more and in different ways, and had upset me more. I think the people I dealt with genuinely wanted to end their life for various reasons personal to them but for me it was confusion and my mind playing tricks on me. Not only that but it was desperation for that feeling of no longer being me to go away. We talked about the incidents and how they had affected me which gently led us on to talking about what I had done to myself recently. It felt the right time to speak about it. She asked opened questions as she wanted me to open up and have a proper think about it all. It was so hard though as I couldn't make sense of it myself. I literally had no idea why my behaviour had got so out of control. That was the worst thing about it all, not being able to pin point or have a reason for it all, which was scary in a way as I was worried that if I got better what was stopping it from happening again. If I couldn't find a cause, how was I completely going to fix it and stay well.

I tried my best to explain things, telling her that I would be okay one minute and then I would suddenly get overwhelmed by it all and completely lose touch with reality. I often got warning signs, including depression, extreme anxiety, feeling 'different' or that my thoughts that I was dying had sped up. The feelings were vague and hard to understand and extremely scary. I think for me the worst thing was feeling depersonalised in that I didn't feel like myself and felt detached from situations. I had no reason to want to harm myself but all these emotions made me believe that there was no other option and that it was my only way out if I wanted them to end and get some peace. That's all I wanted was peace and for my brain to not think anymore. It's tyring thinking that you're going to die and you genuinely believe it despite every professional and family member telling you otherwise. The feeling is that overwhelming and real that absolutely no one could convince you otherwise.

If only someone had sat me down at the time, especially when I was sectioned and explained psychosis to me then maybe, just maybe I could have tried to make sense of things a bit more instead of thinking I had completely gone mad for no reason. I personally believe that if you can put a label to things, it can help you to recover. My counsellor seemed to nod in all the right places and probed me at times to go into more depth about certain things. I was describing how I felt only weeks ago and, in some circumstances, I still felt these symptoms, maybe not on as large a scale as the day I was sectioned but I still felt detached a lot of the time. We ended this session with her going further back, before my breakdown. She said she wanted to try and get me to think about why I had taken the breakdown of my relationship so bad and what I thought had caused it all to go so badly. In all honesty I had no idea at the time. I had my thoughts on why my brain crashed, the main one being the medication I was put on. I was given pill after pill in the hope that one of them would stabilise me and in the end, I think my brain was pumped that full of them that it crashed and gave up. Part of me believes that I had an allergic reaction to a specific medication I was given. Substance-induced psychosis (commonly known as toxic psychosis) is a form of psychosis that is attributed to substance use. It is a psychosis that results from the effects of chemicals or drugs, including those produced by the body itself. I will never be able to prove this now but had I been tested at the time then maybe something might have shown up and I could have been treated properly and looked after rather than shoved away and pumped full of even more drugs that were responsible for it in the first place.

The only other theory I have is that my brief psychosis was caused by extreme stress and the traumatic loss of my Nanna and also the breakdown of my long-term relationship. I find this theory hard to believe though as I have been through so much more loss since then including my dad which I will talk about later. Although this was horrific and devastating, I coped with it and never had a relapse. I wasn't and haven't been on any type of medication for thirteen years now so maybe that's why things were different. The counsellor advised me that I would probably never fully get the answers I so much wanted but that it would hopefully help me if I had reasons to fall back on rather than always searching for something I may never find.

This particular session was hard as I had really tested my brain and I slept for hours when I got home. In fact, I didn't have the energy for anything for the next couple of days. I had to pluck the energy up from somewhere though as I had received a letter that week advising me that I needed to attend a welfare conference at the police headquarters the following Monday to discuss my future with the constabulary. I had been dreading this letter as it was easier to just think of myself as a police officer on a very long career break and convince myself I would go back some day. Monday could completely change that and matters could be taken out of my hands. I was scared that they were going to see me as a lost cause and give up on me, like the two bosses that had come to the house. My job, my career, was the one main thing that was making me fight to get better. Even if I had no hope of wearing that uniform again, the thought of it gave me the motivation and strength I needed to keep going. I didn't want anyone to take that away from me just yet as I would be left with nothing to aim towards which terrified me as it may make me give up completely.

CHAPTER TWENTY-NINE

I was still avoiding my friends at this point so what chance did I have of sitting in a room full of people, discussing my mental health and the unrealistic prospect of a return date to such a responsible and important role. I couldn't look after myself still so what hope did I have of looking after other people. I knew I had to go though so when Monday arrived, I put on my best pair of pants, just about squeezing into them as I had put so much weight on and tried to remain as focussed as I could. My mum and dad drove me there but waited in the car for me. As much as I wanted them to come in and hold my hand, I knew I had to do this on my own. I had to show them that I was still a functioning adult, to some degree, and taking my parents into a meeting would not come across well at all. It was an horrendous feeling walking into that room and knowing that I would have to be as honest as I could without being too honest so that I talked myself out of my career. No, I wasn't better yet, and no I wouldn't be able to function at work just yet but I needed to give them a bit of hope too and enough evidence for them to believe in me and keep my job open just a little bit longer.

The meeting was chaired by the Assistant Chief Constable (ACC) and the usual note taker, HR and my Fed Rep (union) were present. There was no one from my previous place of work as they had already made it pretty clear that I was no longer welcome there. I was hoping that they were up to speed on the background of everything so I didn't need to go through it all. Luckily for me they were. The ACC started with introductions and then went straight on to asking me how I was and if there was anything that the constabulary could do to help me. She was so understanding and sympathetic about what I had been through and in fact the most understanding anyone had been at all. No judgements or making me feel like I had been a burden in any way, just sincere concerns and offers of help. I really needed this so I decided to go down the honest route, I would be lying if I said I was well and ready to come back. Instead, I explained briefly how traumatic it had all been, but that the last few weeks since starting counselling and reducing my medication, I had slowly started to turn a corner. I explained that I was eager to get back to work and have some routine and normality in my life but I just needed a little more time to ensure that I was completely fit to come back. We discussed the fact that it would not be good for my health to return to my previous division. We were all in agreeance with that and I was told that I could pick where I wanted to go. The

ACC said there was no pressure or time limit and that my job was safe and going nowhere, as long as I was heading in the right direction with my recovery which I was and I had convinced them of this. I have often thought about that meeting and how that one boss helped me in ways she will never know. She gave me the confidence and strength to keep going and, not only that, she treated me like a human being that had just had a blip in her life, not like some nutter, like other people in the force have made me feel like. She was one of the people that not only helped me that day but in my recovery as a whole.

I left that meeting feeling like I had a bit of a plan in my head and feeling hopeful again, a feeling that I had forgotten and so longed for. You take these things for granted when you're well and living a 'normal' life but when you experience something major in your life and literally stare death in the face, as I had, you cherish these moments and want them to last forever. I now needed to carry on getting better. As much as I wanted to get that uniform back on and fight crime, I had no idea how my muddled brain was going to cope with it, not yet anyway.

The atmosphere at home was different that night. The positive meeting had had a positive effect on all of us and it was good to see a smile on my mum and dad's face for once, something that I had been longing to see for some time now. They too felt a glimmer of hope that they were slowly getting their daughter back on the road to her recovery and her life in general. I wasn't getting giddy or ahead of myself as I knew I still had a few hard months ahead of me and I always had the worry at the back of my mind of a relapse. Something I had to live with for many years. However, I tried my best to push this to the back of my head that night and attempted to enjoy that feeling a little longer.

My counselling had come round again and today's session consisted of yet another chat about another horrible death I had dealt with. In fact, I think we covered two in this session. The first one being a female, that I found at her home address, and there was evidence of her having attempted various methods to take her own life before finally throwing herself off her balcony at the top of her stairs and she was swinging on a rope. Her house was like a crime scene. In the upstairs bathroom were empty packets of tablets laid out or should I say scattered around as though they had been emptied in a hurry. There were a lot and she had made a serious attempt for this to have been her cause of death, unlike me that time. I'm guessing these tablets hadn't worked as quick as she'd wanted so she then tried to cut her wrists, again the evidence of blood all over the bathroom sink and floor and on her wrists which I had noticed as soon as I had seen her hanging there. Being a professional woman which I later found out she was, this was probably the first time she had contemplated ending her life and trying these things. She didn't know exactly where abouts to cut her wrist to have the effect she was aiming for so that hadn't worked either, other than cause her a lot of pain and even more panic during her frenzied attack to end it all. Unlike my attempts, she was totally serious about killing herself and it was far from a cry for help. She wanted to check out and tried every way possible before building up the courage to throw herself off the balcony. I say courage, as it must take a lot of mental strength and desperation to do something like that. When I tied things round my neck, I never had the capacity to go any further as the thought of not being in this world terrified me even though I wanted it all to end and go away. Maybe even then I hung on to the fact that I had the strength to get better and beat the beast trapped inside my head.

I did what I needed to do and waited for the cavalry to arrive to do their bit and for her to get cut down and taken away to the mortuary. It felt so undignified to watch. What could have gone so wrong in this poor woman's life for it to have ended so quickly and so brutally. Maybe she had suffered a psychotic breakdown like me. Who knows, and that's just it, we very rarely got to find out. We turn up as cops to these situations and deal with them the best way and most respectful way we can and then are expected to just move on to the next job and put that one in a box and try to forget about it, something I found hard to do throughout all of my career. These were people at the end of the day, human beings, someone's daughter, mum, friend, colleague. I always thought about jobs in that way, no matter what I was dealing with. That's why things probably affected me a lot more than my colleagues who could just detach themselves and move on. Part of me wanted to be like them but I'm glad I wasn't in another sense as it made me care more and I never wanted to get 'used' to these situations and become desensitised.

When she was finally placed in the back of the private ambulance by the undertakers, I was told to just lock up and bring the key back to the nick. Another thing I disliked about these jobs. We often just left the scenes as we found them minus the body. I couldn't imagine walking into this house, as one of this female's loved ones, and finding it in this state. They would be horrified. No one should have to endure seeing her desperate attempts and her blood splattered about the bathroom. Nor should they have to clean up her vomit or faeces on the hall floor from when she jumped and her body gave up. I know it wasn't in my job description either but I would rather do it, being that bit more detached, than subject them to it. I didn't give the house a complete makeover but I made sure all evidence in the bathroom was removed, the tablet packets had to be seized for the coroner anyway, but I made sure the vomit and blood was cleaned up as best as possible. I did the same in the hallway too. Don't get me wrong, although I was detached from the situation this is still a hard task to carry out and you can't under estimate the effect that it has on you at that time and afterwards. Police officers are still human beings at the end of the day and aren't taught how to deal with things like this in training. To be a good cop in the first place though you have to have compassion and I think that's what sends you into over drive in these situations and gets you through it. I never told anyone what I had done that day as I didn't want a lecture about it not being my job and that I was needed back out on the streets to respond to the next emergency. I just did it and was glad I did as I felt I made that horrific situation just that tiny bit easier for her loved ones.

My counsellor picked up on bits throughout my recollection of this event, in particular asking how it made me feel seeing her hanging and what thoughts were going through my head clearing up at the end. It was so long ago it was hard to explain or remember how I felt, however, I know I still felt quite anxious reliving this particular job. You think you've dealt with the emotions involved with jobs like this, even if you've relived them in your head for a week or so, but in reality, all you really do is bury them deep inside your brain and they lay dormant for years just waiting to pop up again. I often found that a certain smell or something on the TV could remind you of that situation in an instance which was such a weird feeling.

We briefly talked about another death I had been to but not a suicide this time. It was an accidental drowning of a young male. He had been on a stag do with his friends and decided it was a good idea to jump into the sea late at night after drinking all day, a recipe for disaster. Again, like the murder months before, I was first on scene. The weather was horrific which made it virtually impossible to establish where he was. I eventually manged to locate one of his friends and he showed me where he had entered the sea. This didn't really help though as it had been at least half an hour since he had gone in there. After scanning the sea with my bog-standard police issue Maglite, I saw something bobbing up in the sea yards away from where I was stood on the promenade. There it was again and I knew this time that it was him. I lowered myself down so that I was lying on my front which gave me more leverage to be able to pull him out if I could reach him. However, it was impossible, the waves were so forceful that night that they kept sweeping him back under like a blanket wrapped around his body. I made one last attempt to grab hold of his hand which was literally inches away from mine but the waves came again and he was gone and this time he wasn't coming back up, at least alive anyway. Being so near to saving someone was horrendous and I kept mulling it over in my mind, if I'd positioned myself slightly more to the left or right or edged out that bit more could I have saved him. The reality was I couldn't, and I think I knew that but you can't help being self-critical in these situations. Although this job has stuck in my head for various reasons it didn't affect me as much as the other two jobs, the murder and suicide we had already discussed. Yes, it was devastating for the family and wasn't pleasant to deal with but it wasn't as horrific and gruesome as the others.

I left the counselling session that day wondering again why we hadn't talked about my breakdown or how I was feeling now, rather than just about jobs that had affected me six years ago. She was the professional though and I had to trust she had a plan and that things would start to knit into place over the coming weeks. I only had five sessions booked which doesn't seem like a lot but is pretty average unless your counsellor feels you need more. So, I had two more left which I presumed would be the knitting together of everything. I was happy with how things were going though as one I had stuck with it so far and two, I genuinely felt like it was helping.

CHAPTER THIRTY

The following week was a bit up and down in the respect of my emotions and motivation. I knew I was going to have high and lows still and I was always worse at the beginning of the week after my session. As the week went on, I decided to pluck up the courage and meet my best friend who had so desperately wanted to see me for weeks but I kept putting her off as I didn't have the energy nor want her to see me like this. This was a big step for me as I was forcing myself back out there and it made me feel quite vulnerable. The night before our meet I contemplated cancelling on numerous occasions but stopped myself as I knew I had to do this if I stood any chance of getting back to work any time soon.

She came to my house the next day and I couldn't help thinking whether she would be shocked to see me and what I had turned in to. I hadn't seen her for a while, even prior to my breakdown, so the last time she saw me I was the athletic framed Beck who exercised five times a week and looked after myself. Not the overweight, scruffy Beck that I had become. Nevertheless, if she was shocked, she hid it well and tried to be upbeat with me. It was so good to see her but it was also hard hearing about what she had been up to and how her normal life had continued whilst mine had fallen apart. I couldn't dwell on this though and when she asked me how I was I just shrugged my shoulders and said I was getting there. I was lost for words and found it so difficult to make conversation as I literally had nothing to talk about or anything of any interest. I mean who would find my life interesting as all I did was sit in my room, go to my counselling and eat, three dull topics which I didn't want to bore her with. We ended up going out for a drive and parking up at the top of a hill nearby. We talked about rubbish and reminisced about our childhood and growing up together and it was nice to talk about topics other than my illness, which had consumed me for months. I actually switched off for an hour or so and dare I say it relaxed. We said we would do it again soon but made no firm plans as I didn't know how I was going to feel from one minute to the next let alone next week. I'm so glad I pushed myself that day as it's so easy to say no to people when you're in that mindset and stay in your comfort zone but when you've done it, you're glad you made the effort.

The rest of that week I decided I would try and do something each day, no matter how small or insignificant it was, I would do it. It was only little things, like go for a drive or walk with my mum and dad or get up and dressed before a certain time. Boring mundane things that had once been second nature to me. I remember going on those walks, as all I did was say I was dying whilst we plodded along, my mum and dad trying to reassure me I wasn't. Although I was getting slightly better and hadn't had another 'episode' I was still convinced that I had a life- threatening illness and that no one was willing to help me. Even after months of getting out of hospital this thought was still there and still felt very real. In fact, it probably took years to fully go, even when I was back leading a functional life. I had to retrain my brain to think differently.

In the March of that year, it was my 30th birthday, a significant one and one I would have celebrated and milked for months had I been well. My sister was nearing the end of her first pregnancy with my first niece or nephew. I had always wanted to be an auntie and I so desperately wanted to be full of excitement and joy but I wasn't, I still felt numb when it came to special things like these. So, the day of my birthday came and unbelievably the birth of my first niece. Of all the days she happened to be born on my special birthday. How amazing and special and I would have been ecstatic if I'd been well. Don't get me wrong, I was happy, course I was, but not as happy as I should have been. This made me feel extremely sad as it was another reality check that I was still very unwell and another important event in my life that I couldn't enjoy like I wanted to, despite trying so hard. The only thing I did for my birthday was a family meal with one of my friends who had never stopped supporting me throughout all this. Not the big party I would have liked but I had to mark it in some way, for my parents' sake more than mine as all I wanted to do was go home and be on my own.

That week was a turning point for me though as I realised my only option was to get better. I needed to get better so I could enjoy my new beautiful niece and she could get to know her fun auntie, not the zombie auntie I still was. I don't want that to come across in the wrong way because it's never as easy as just 'choosing' to get better. Mental health is a very complex thing. It's indescribable and excruciatingly painful to make that step to choose to get better. It's a choice to talk to people, it's a choice to take medication, and it's so hard to do that. To fight to stay alive? That is the bravest thing any human being can do.

CHAPTER THIRTY-ONE

The visits to the local doctor's surgery started to become less frequent but I still went with every lump and bump I found or any other symptom I thought was a sign that I was dying. I talked about all this in my second to last counselling session. My counsellor never asked me about work during this session but started it off by asking me why I was convinced I was dying and that the NHS were ignoring my life-threatening illness. Even writing these words today seems like utter madness so I'm sure those reading it will probably think the same. I told her that I had always been a sensitive person growing up and somewhat of a worrier. I never really had anything to worry about during my childhood or even my teen years but I would find silly little things to fret about. Obviously starting a career in the police at twenty-two years old was daunting and I witnessed things in that first year that no one should ever have to see let alone someone so young, but I think at the time I took it in my stride and just got on with it. You have to as a police officer or you'd just lose the plot straight away. So where had this thought about me dying emerged from and so deeply embedded in my brain. The answer to that question was that I had absolutely no idea whatsoever. We talked about everything building up to my 'episode' again, the sudden loss of my dear Nanna and the breakdown of my long- term relationship which I had ultimately caused, but I was still none the wiser. She still confirmed that this could be a contributing factor.

She then ran through the tablets that I was prescribed at the time, specifically commenting on the fact that I was on a lot of medication and had a lot of changes with the type and dose that I was on leading up to it. I explained to her that although I was confused and starting to spiral out of control, I went significantly worse when I was put on all these drugs and that I genuinely believed they were the reason for my breakdown. She confirmed that the medication I was put on was a major contributing factor to my psychosis. I know I touched on it earlier but research has shown that 'drug induced psychosis is often caused by taking too much of a certain drug, so that its level of toxicity provokes paranoia (in my case I was dying and it was being covered up) and a psychotic episode'. It can also occur if you have an adverse reaction from mixing different substances, or withdrawing from a drug, prescribed or otherwise. The symptoms of drug induced psychosis are often gradual, which is what happened to me. I went deeper and deeper into that black hole very slowly. My medication was upped and upped when I wasn't showing any signs of improvement which, again, research has shown that the toxicity of the drug becomes more dangerous as the frequency and the dosage of the drug increases with dependency. I wasn't particular dependent on the drugs that were given to me but I took them as I trusted the people that prescribed me them and trusted that they would help, when in fact they sent me into my psychotic breakdown.

It's only whilst doing research for this book that I have come to believe that this is what happened to me. It makes total sense as before I was placed on this medication, I was okay. I'm not saying that the trauma of the other two events didn't contribute in some way, they probably did but I'm now, finally content that I have an answer to why this happened to me. I know it doesn't change things but it is comforting to have a reason for it in my own head and makes me believe that this won't happen again. It was an isolated time in my life and to this day I have never come close to anything like this again despite suffering trauma in my life since. It's the only explanation that makes sense to me as I was fine before and have been fine since getting better about twelve years ago. Had this even been a consideration or picked up at the beginning by the numerous doctors I saw then maybe I might have been treated and dealt with differently. And who knows maybe I would never have got carted off to that hell hole and pumped full of more drugs that contributed to the continued psychosis I went through and added trauma. I know I would have been poorly still and needed to be monitored closely and weaned off my medication but surely there would have been a better place to do this rather than locking me up and drugging me up. To this day I am still paranoid about medication and don't take anything until I have completely researched it and am satisfied that it won't harm me in any way. I am probably too over cautious but I'd rather be like that and remain well than ever go anywhere near that living nightmare ever again.

CHAPTER THIRTY-TWO

We discussed all this during the session and she confirmed again that the medication could have been a major contributing factor to my psychotic episode. She then went on to discuss how she felt that the traumatic jobs I had dealt with so early on in my career could also have been a contributing factor and it was then that she gave me the diagnosis of PTSD. Back then and so early on in my career I didn't really give this much thought but since she mentioned it, she may have been right. Again, I'm not saying that this caused my episode but even to this day, I think about these particular jobs now and again and maybe witnessing them gave me the specific ideas of how I acted out my cries for help.

I had one more counselling session left but I asked her if we could leave it for now as I felt that I was talked to death and didn't want to over- do it, plus I felt like I was in an okay place. She agreed and told me that I could come back anytime. She went through some self- help therapies that I could take with me and use if my anxiety ever occurred, which I used a lot over the coming months. They were nothing fancy, just breathing exercises and ways for me to calm myself down if I ever felt I was getting stressed or anxious about something. I'd always been cynical about things like that but they actually worked. They're not for everyone and you have to adopt a style that suits yourself for it to work, which I did, and you also have to keep an open mind.

So, it had been nearly twelve months now since I was discharged from hospital and although it seemed like yesterday since I was in there, I was in there, I realised how far I had come in that time. I had now been off work almost seventeen months as I was off a period of time building up to my episode. I was far from better but I knew I had to bite the bullet and get myself back to work. It was big step, in fact a huge step to take and looking back I can't believe I did it but I knew that if I didn't do it now then I never would. This was the best decision I made so far as I can honestly say it saved me in the end. When I say I was far from better, I mean in the sense of my confidence and self-esteem, which to hit rock bottom with these things, it takes a long time to get them back and I knew that the only way to do this was get back out into the big world and relearn everything again. Yes, it was a gamble as it could have backfired on me, especially going back to such a serious and responsible job but I had to give it a shot. I figured with the skills I had learnt in counselling and the continued support from my family and friends I stood a good chance.

I had picked where I wanted to work not long after my welfare meeting. I picked this particular place because I didn't know anyone there, which may seem strange but I wanted a complete fresh start where no one knew about my past. I'm not naïve, as cops love gossip and I was under no illusions that the odd person would know about me but it was a lot better than returning to my old haunt and constantly worrying and being gossiped about. I contacted my fed rep and a date was arranged for me to return to work, something I worked so hard for and never in a million years thought would happen. I was still on medication at this point but it had dramatically been reduced and I was literally only on anti-depressants by this point. I wanted to knock these on the head as well but on the advice of my doctor continued taking them for the time being. I still felt slightly detached from reality but my brain fog was so much better since coming off all the other drugs that I had been taking. Lack of brain fog also meant that I could start driving again which was one of the biggest steps in my recovery as I finally had some independence back. It took a while for me to get my confidence back up, but it gave me a new lease of life and I actually wanted to get out and about again, plus I needed this to be able to return to work which gave me the push I needed.

Monday morning arrived, my first day back at work in a completely new division after eighteen months off and having suffered the biggest trauma in my life. To say it was daunting is an understatement but I pulled on my big girl pants and went for it. I was on a phased return for a while so only had to go in for four hours which doesn't seem a lot but four minutes even felt long when you weren't used to it. After all it wasn't that long ago that taking a shower or getting dressed was a mammoth task, so standing here in my uniform amongst more than two people felt like I had walked up Everest. It was a bit of an admin day that day and meeting my team. They must have wondered what I was all about as I hardly spoke. It felt so strange being back in a busy place with people all around me and all I wanted to do was make a run for it, get back in my car and go home and hide away in my bedroom. I knew today was a big day but I didn't realise it would be as scary as it was. I took myself off to the toilets and sat there doing my breathing exercises trying to calm myself down which actually worked. I had a quiet word with myself and got back out there and met my new supervisor which, I have to say, was lovely. She made me feel welcome and stressed to me that I could take things at my own pace for a while as she knew I had been off a long time. She never mentioned anything about my past and to be honest I don't even think she had been told the ins and outs about it all which made things a lot easier for me. She would have obviously been told something as she would need to keep an eye on me but I was grateful that she wasn't told everything. It was my story to tell at the end of the day and even now I haven't told that many people, obviously until now. At first, I wanted to keep it quiet because of the shame of it all but now, fifteen years later, I have learnt that there is nothing to be ashamed of and if anything, I am proud of how far I have come and the strength I have shown.

I got through those four hours by the skin of my teeth, but I did it. I was actually back at work in my uniform and a police officer again. I would never have thought fifteen months ago whilst sat in hospital that this day would actually come. Maybe my life would actually return to normal one day and I would get the old Beck back once and for all. It was baby steps though as I was still a shell of my former self and I knew I needed to dig deep each day and find that motivation to keep going. I went back though the next day and the next day after that and kept on going back. Some days I literally had to drag myself out of bed and some days I just sat in my car on the car park forcing myself to get out as the fear of being around people engulfed me. I did it though, I have no idea how, but I did it. Before I knew it, I was back up to six hours a day and finally allowed back out on the streets in company with someone. I had been back four weeks now and although it was scary to think I would be going to jobs again, jobs that were once second nature to me, I just went with the flow. We only attended easy jobs at first, when I say easy, I mean your bog-standard shop lifter or burglary. I appreciated that they were trying their best to ease me back into things slowly and keep me way from traumatic situations for the time being. Gradually over the weeks my confidence and self-esteem started to come back little by little. It felt amazing. I was able to make conversation with people again and actually started talking to my colleagues and dare I say it, laughed! I had missed laughing so much and it felt like an eternity since I had found anything remotely funny. Don't get me wrong, I'm not saying I was cured and I still had that dreaded feeling that I was dying but during the six hours I was at work I was able to put that to the back of my head as I now had something else to think about and concentrate on. I was still paranoid to hell about whether people really knew what had happened to me and thought I was some nutter, but I just had to get on with it all and hope for the best.

CHAPTER THIRTY-THREE

Before I knew it, I had been back at work six months attending job after job and was now working on my own. It was strange really how quickly I fitted back in. I was still attending my regular checkups at the hospital to monitor my medication but I was actually leading near enough a normal life in terms of my independence, confidence and interaction with the public and my colleagues and friends. Six months probably seems a short time to have gained all these qualities back but I had to work really hard at it. I read self- help books in my spare time and just learnt how to look after myself again. I started running again, something that slipped away from me when I got poorly and missed more than anything. This had a huge effect on my mental health and made me feel so much more positive about life in general and especially more so when I stated to lose all that weight that I had gained from the medication. I was still being picky about what jobs I went to as I didn't want to push myself and there was still that niggling feeling at the back of my head that worried me. I was worried that if I attended a traumatic incident would it send me back to that awful place? Would I be able to cope with it? I guess you don't know until you're in that situation but for the time being I wasn't going to chance it. I was doing so well and didn't want anything to potentially jeopardise it.

Life at my mum and dads became a much happier place and they too were now able to resume their lives which was so good to see as they had put their life on hold for the last two years to look after me. I can't imagine how it had been for them to have watched me go through all this and I always remember my mum saying that she thought she would lose me one day. No mum should have to go through that and endure that pain. I knew I had to make them proud and by me getting my life back, I was doing just that, and this was the only thing they wanted. This gave me the strength to keep going over the next coming months and years and before I knew it, I was eighty per cent back to my normal self. The twenty per cent being that I still had that dreaded thought of dying hanging over me like a black cloud, but all I could do was hope that it would go eventually and if not, that I would learn to live with it as best I could.

The months rolled on and before I knew it, I had been back at work eight months and was starting to put myself forward for bigger jobs. I wanted to test myself and see how far I had actually come so responded to probably the biggest, most important, call yet since returning to work. A call had been received from staff at the local psych ward about one of the residents kicking off and they needed Police assistance. A number of my colleagues shouted up and there was actually no need for me to attend as they had enough. However, I knew I couldn't put it off forever as there may just be me clear next time and able to attend, so at least my colleagues would be there this time in order for me to test things out. As I drove there all my memories came flooding back in an instant and my anxiety levels were already on the rise. How would I feel stepping back in one of these places again? What if there was a staff member working there now that recognised me? I felt physically sick. Breathe Beck, breathe, I kept saying to myself, you can do this.

As I pulled up outside yet another drab, prehistoric looking concrete building, I noticed that no one else was here yet and I was first on scene. There was a member of staff already waiting by the main door to let us in. I froze for a minute just staring at him thinking how I could get out of going in there. The reality was, I couldn't. Like my colleagues, this member of staff knew nothing about what happened to me, they didn't know that just under two years ago that this was me living in one of these places. All he saw was a police officer sat in the car, with a moment of hesitation, stalling to get out. He was waving me over as if to say hurry up you're needed. One of my colleagues had arrived thank God and before I knew it, I was walking down that long bleak corridor. Obviously not the same one but they all look alike in these places, with the bleak bare walls and the smell of disinfectant. I could already hear the screams coming from behind the door and my heart was starting to race so fast and my palms became clammy. I'm not ashamed to admit it but I was absolutely terrified, and despite wearing this uniform I was back to that vulnerable scared girl again. A feeling that I had not missed in the slightest and hoped I wouldn't feel again. However, the reality was, it was happening, I was there to help so I had to get on with it and deal with my feelings after it was done. The doors swung open at the end of the corridor, and there it was, as I had predicted in my mind. Some poor individual lying face down on the concrete floor with four members of staff on top of him pinning him down. Breathe Beck, breathe! I managed to go into cop mode and placed myself on the floor near his head. Yes, he was kicking off but for what reason we had not yet been told. It was all a bit manic to be honest and in between the swearing and shouting from both him and the staff, I just about managed to figure out that he had tried to make a run for it when staff had gone out of the door. I didn't blame him, I thought, as I would have done the same given the chance. It was so strange being on the other side of this situation as all I wanted to do was side with the male that was kicking off and get him out of there but I knew I couldn't and I had to help the staff, however much as I resented that. I know there are good and bad staff in every work place but my own personal experience of these places there were more bad, than good.

Memories were still flooding back and I had to concentrate more than ever if I was going to get through the next hour without having a complete melt down, and finally letting my secret out to my colleagues. I tried my best to calm him down but all he kept saying to me was I didn't understand. If only he knew, because I more than understood what he was going through right now. He told me that he was sick of being drugged up and wanted out, again something that unfortunately I could relate to so much. I could see my colleagues rolling their eyes at each other and were probably thinking he was some kind of nutter and to be honest I probably would have been the same at one time. However, I wasn't anymore. Once you've been on that side and experienced it you have so much more understanding and compassion for people going through similar situations. I don't blame my colleagues for their eye rolling as they didn't understand, how could they. They trusted what the staff were telling them, like my parents trusted them, where as I trusted him more and what he was saying. Staff had informed us that he had tried to escape out of the doors and when stopped had become violent with them which meant they had to physically restrain him and inject him with a sedative to calm him down which clearly hadn't worked due to the size of him. That same sedative that had been injected into my buttock time and time again but unlike him had worked and completely knocked me out.

Staff were contemplating another injection but I asked them if I could try and talk to him first before they did.

He was still thrashing about a bit but had calmed down slightly and seemed to be engaging with me. I asked the staff to release their pressure slightly as I could see that they were starting to hurt him despite his solid frame. They did as I asked but I could see by their faces that they weren't happy and thought I was taking over. They had called us after all so the least they could do was give us the courtesy of trying to calm him down before drugging him up again which I knew they were dying to do. This might be a different psych unit but I was quickly starting to realise that it applied the same tactics. I guess I was biased now after everything and part of me wondered if they were justified in what they were doing but I couldn't shake off the feeling that it wasn't right and after all I had seen this done so many times on both myself and other residents that were completely unjustified. I don't think I will ever trust staff in these places ever again. I talked to the male for a while and tried to get him to realise that the more he kicked off the worse he would be treated, if only I had had someone tell me that. It took a while but eventually he stopped resisting as the penny must have dropped that he was fighting a losing battle, that along with the exhaustion of kicking off for the past hour. With the help of staff, we escorted him back into his room and his door was locked, the staff advising us that it was only temporarily whilst he got some rest. I beg to differ, as who knows what happened to him once we left, I suspect another load of drugs would be forced down him.

As myself and my colleagues walked down the corridor towards the exit I suddenly got overwhelmed again. The feeling was so intense that I felt like I could pass out at any given moment. I saw some toilets near the exit so I darted into them telling them I would see them back at the nick later. I locked myself in the cubicle and sat down on the floor, sweat dripping down my head by this point and my heart feeling like it was going to explode. I genuinely thought I was having a heart attack. What an earth was happening to me I thought as the inside of the cubicle was spinning like I was in a washing machine. It was then that I experienced my first panic attack. I thought anxiety was bad but that had nothing on a full-blown panic attack. It was horrendous. I shut my eyes and took deep breaths attempting to calm myself down but it didn't seem to be working. I genuinely felt like I was going to pass out. I sat there for a while with my head between my legs panting like a dog. This was ridiculous, I knew it would affect me in some way but this was bad, very bad. Coming back into one of these places had crippled me and I was so worried that my life as a cop was over. If I couldn't deal with a situation like this, then what future did I have. I tried to rationalise it all and eventually I started to calm down and my breathing started to return to normal. I put my stab vest back on which I had literally ripped off me and thrown on the floor as I thought it was restricting my breathing. I pulled myself together and made a dash for the exit and into my car. Luckily all my colleagues had left. I was still shaking and felt physically sick so quickly pulled off the car park and onto a quiet lane at the side of the hospital. It is then that I started to uncontrollably sob and couldn't stop. I was an absolute mess. My first major wobble since being back at work and I hated it. I hadn't formed any real close friendships with anyone on my team by this point or told a soul about my past so there was no one I could ring to come to me and help me calm down. I didn't want to ring my parents as I didn't want to burst that happy, content bubble that they were now in and give them reason to worry about me. Therefore, I knew I had to deal with it on my own and that is exactly what I did. I just sat there with my eyes closed and concentrated on my breathing, reliving the techniques that I had gone over and over in my bedroom at home. I'm glad I had practised these so much as eventually it worked and I was back in the room, albeit looking a complete mess but I was with it again. I was now faced with the decision of whether to just put this down as a bad experience and get on with it or tell someone and get some help. I knew if I told someone I could risk being put back in the office or monitored closely again but I also knew that by not telling someone or dealing with it I ran the risk of it happening again.

When I finally felt fit to drive, I drove back to the nick and asked my supervisor if I could have a quick word. I didn't go into any great detail but explained that I had struggled at that last job and asked if I could go home as I needed to get myself together. This was the first time since being back that I had asked to leave and the first time that I had had to admit that I had struggled with something so she was extremely understanding and told me to take the next day off in order for me to speak to someone if I needed to. I know I mentioned earlier that I didn't think she knew stuff about me but after leaving her office that day I was under the impression that she knew more than I thought. Her discretion about it all made me respect her all the more. As soon as I got in my car, I rang my counsellor to make an appointment and luckily, she had one free the next day. I saw it as a bit of a backwards step having to go and see her again after all this time but I knew it was the right thing to do. I just needed to touch base and make sense of what had happened to me today so that I could carry on as normal.

CHAPTER THIRTY-FOUR

It seemed like ages ago since I was sat back in her room and she greeted me telling me how well I looked which was good to hear as I didn't feel it as the panic attack had left me feeling drained. I talked through the job with her and how I felt from when I arrived on scene to leaving and then having what I thought was a panic attack. She asked me to describe my symptoms and how I felt and without any hesitation or thought she confirmed that I had had a full-on panic attack. She explained that panic attacks weren't to be underestimated and genuinely make people feel like they are dying. I knew that's what had happened to me but it was reassuring to hear it from her. Since my psychotic episode and that dreaded on going feeling I was dying, I suppose I was still very paranoid about things and terrified of something happening to me again. We talked about ways for me to deal with it should it happen again, which it probably would, and she also advised me to maybe avoid these situations for a while which was easier said than done when you're out there being dictated to by the radio. She explained that it was completely normal for me to have experienced these feelings, having set foot back into place where I had endured so much trauma less than two years ago. Even now if I see these places on the TV, I have to turn it off as I can't mentally deal with it, and that's fifteen years on, so no wonder it affected me so badly then when it was still so raw.

I was glad I went to counselling that day as, although she couldn't fix it or promise me, I wouldn't have another, she reassured me that it was perfectly normal. Being and feeling normal was something I needed to hear as it had taken me a long time to feel even close to this again. I went back to work the next day and updated my supervisor that I had got my head together and was okay and she took my word for it and let me resume my duties as normal. We had developed a mutual trust quite quickly and I think she knew I would be honest with her now if I felt I was struggling.

Throughout the next year I grew and grew in confidence and although I managed to avoid going back to the psych unit again, I started to gravitate towards mental health related jobs. Any jobs involving people threatening to jump off a building, to parents ringing in about their sons or daughters'self-harming, I would be there. I wanted to go to these jobs as I felt I could make a difference. I'm not saying my colleagues were no good at communicating with these people but I knew, to a certain extent, how they must be feeling and how desperate they were, and I wanted to help them. I guess you could say I could relate to them and their desperation. Those kinds of jobs were often dealt with as a team due the persons unpredictable behaviour. However once that person had been talked down and taken to A&E, or left at home with parents, most of the team resumed and went to other jobs. It was then, when I was on my own, that I would share my experience with them. It may seem a little unprofessional but I felt that telling them my story, and how I got better and was stood there now in front of them in my uniform, might give them a bit of hope. I remember when I was going through it all, how lonely and isolated it felt and that no one understood, not even the professionals. Yes, people can say they understand and offer that advice and reassurance but I genuinely believe that only those people that have experienced it first-hand know exactly how it feels. That is no disrespect to people trying to help, it's just how it is. You have to go through such a bad time in your life and feel that low to fully appreciate how bad it actually feels.

I'd finally found something good to have come out of my bad situation, that it had made me a better cop. I was always a good listener and fair before everything happened, but if I was being completely honest, I never fully understood mental health and often thought that the people we turned up to at jobs were either completely barking or attention seekers. Even those that call up week after week just wanting attention and seemingly wasting police time, I had more time for. These people have ended up being like this for a reason and I genuinely believe that every person has a story and has got to where they have for their own reasons that need to be listened to and respected no matter how small or insignificant they seem. Previously I would have got annoyed at these types of people and couldn't wait to rush off to the next job, whereas now I listened even if I did think they were speaking nonsense. Sometimes poorly people just want to be heard, nothing more, nothing less, just heard.

It wasn't just mental health jobs that interested me, it was any job that involved helping people in a crisis and it wasn't long before I applied to become a trained Family Liaison Officer working alongside the Force Major Incident Team who ultimately investigated murders and other major incidents. My role was to work with the families who had lost loved ones in the most horrific circumstances. I would be responsible for relaying information to the family and investigation team and to ensure the family received the best care and respect throughout the investigation. It was such a hard role, intruding on a family's grief as it was about to unfold, however I felt I could give something back to that family. Again, I know what I went through was completely different and no one had died but I came close to it and it could have easily turned out different. I knew what grief was from so many different angles, in particular the grief I have since learnt my family suffered when they were losing their daughter and sister right before their eyes and the uncertainty as to whether I'd make it or not.

The demand on mental health jobs grew and grew over the years and I did well to avoid having to go back to the psych unit. There were always calls for the police to assist but I always managed to avoid it somehow. I just couldn't face going back in there again and having another panic attack as I had avoided another one since that day. The only contact I did have with that place was dropping a female off there when I was working nights. She had been on unescorted leave and not returned, so when I eventually found her all I had to do was take her to the main doors where staff were waiting. I remember she was a pleasant girl, poorly like most people are in there, but pleasant. As I got her out of the back of the van, I distinctively remember her saying to me that she didn't want to go back. She wasn't kicking off and was calm when she said it but I will always remember that look of desperation in her eyes as if she wanted saving. I told her it would be okay but all she replied was that I didn't know what when on in these places and that she was sick of being drugged up to the eyeballs and treated like an animal. I tried to reassure her as best I could but she just looked at me like I was any other cop and probably thought I didn't give a damn or understand. I so wish she knew the truth and that I actually believed her. We didn't have the time though as staff were waiting and as I walked her over to the doors, she told me that they gave her a particular drug that erased all her memory. This comment made me freeze on the spot. Was this the same little blue pill that I was always given prior to my parents visiting. I was unable to ask her any more questions as we had reached the doors where staff were stood eagerly waiting. I didn't want to ask anything in front of them and put her in an awkward position or make life in there any harder than it clearly was. It had to be the same pill though. It played on my mind for the rest of that night and all I wanted to do was drive back there and get her and drive her far away from that place. I couldn't though. I couldn't save any of those people in there and I just hoped she found the strength one day like I did, to get better.

CHAPTER THIRTY-FIVE

I'd been back at work now almost two years and the difference in me was unbelievable. I ran on a daily basis and my weight had near enough returned to normal which had a positive effect on both my physical and mental health. I'd been reviewed by my doctor and I had asked if I could come off the last bit of medication I was on. I know this probably seems like a risky thing to do but I wanted to give it a go and be medication free once and for all. I knew if I did it in a controlled way, I would be okay. They agreed to let me give it a try and over the weeks to come decreased it bit by bit and before I knew it, I no longer had to wake up in the morning and take anything. It felt amazing to feel normal again. I know it's not abnormal to take anti-depressants and I know a lot of people on them today, but for me being on them was a big deal as I know this was the cause of my psychosis. So, to be rid of everything in my system, made me feel not only normal but safe. I was medication free three years after my breakdown started and have been medication free ever since. I have not had the need to take any medication of this sort for the past twelve years now.

Although I loved the safety net of living at my parent's house still, I knew it was time to stand on my own two feet again. I had rented my apartment out whilst all this was going on so decided to move back in there. It was a scary move to make as I would be living alone again and would have no one watching over me but I had to do it as it was another part of my recovery process. I hadn't lived with my parents for a while prior to my breakdown and although I will forever be eternally grateful to them it was the right time. I'm not going to pretend it was easy because it wasn't. I often got home at night after work and felt lonely and started to feel those thoughts again that I was dying. Yes, they were still there, lying dormant in my brain ready to pop to the surface at any time. I stuck it out though and eventually things got easier. I think it's like anything, the more you do it the more normal it becomes and things that you once worried about fade into the background.

I had to pinch myself some days as I couldn't believe that three years ago, I was locked up in a secure unit, my whole independence and dignity stripped from me and now I was back at work as a 999-response driver, living on my own again medication free and coping with the day-to-day stresses of life. It felt amazing and quite surreal. In the grand scheme of things, it may have been a short time but it felt like forever ago and it slowly started to feel like it wasn't even me that had experienced it. This was a good feeling as it meant I was finally starting to heal. I still worried at times that my bubble might burst one day and I would have another episode but I knew, in the back of my mind, that to avoid that I just had to stay clear of medication. As time went by, I started to feel less of a 'freak', a 'nutter', both of which I felt for a very long time, in fact years after.

Moving back to my own place gave me the confidence to start dating again and I formed a different couple of relationships with people, some good, some bad. I was always too quick to tell them about my past and probably too much about it too soon. You find that when a relationship isn't going well anymore and is starting to breakdown then your past is dragged up a lot and you end up being the cause for everything even if it is them that have the issues. It's easy to blame someone who has had a past mental health problem and drag things up to make them feel responsible. That is what happened to me during a couple of my relationships. Even though I was fully better they still couldn't help but stick the knife in and remind me of what I went through. I now know that they were deflecting away from their own problems. This only made me put my guard up more and once again I hid my past as best I could through the shame of how I was made to feel.

Although I was ninety-nine-point nine percent sure my psychosis was drug induced there was always that one per cent that worried me that if I suffered another traumatic incident in my life that my brain would crash again. This worry was something I carried around with me every day. I was leading a functional normal 'ish' life by then but it was always there, I never felt fully relaxed or was content with my life. Seven years on from my breakdown this worry was put to the test. My lovely dad, at the age of only sixty-five years, got diagnosed with lung cancer and only three months later, lost his brave battle. No sooner had we been given the news about his diagnosis, then he was gone. As a family we weren't given time to get our heads around the news before having to deal with the loss and grief of his death. Other than my breakdown this was the single most traumatic thing I had experienced in my life. Watching your dad die of such a horrible vicious disease is something I wouldn't wish on anyone. I am only going to touch on this briefly but feel that it is important to share as this was the first time since my breakdown that I had had to go through anything major in my life which put my own resilience to the test.

When I got the news about his diagnosis, I was understandably worried sick about my dad but also myself and how I would handle all this. Last time, when I lost my Nanna, I ended up losing the plot, what if it happened again. The one per cent worry that had always been there was now more like one hundred per cent worry. As the weeks went on and we realised that he was getting very ill very fast, I decided to go off work and move back in with my mum and dad and help look after him. I wanted to spend every second I could with him before he was gone and taken away from me. I am so glad I made this decision as despite his rapid deterioration we were able to make memories in those last weeks and I often got to have honest chats with my dad whilst no one else was around. I would ask him if he was scared and although he said he was at the beginning he said he wasn't anymore and had accepted he was dying. People say that you eventually accept death when you know it's heading your way and my dad did just that. Some days we chatted about nonsense and anything other than the big 'C'. I remember apologising one day to him for everything I had put him through with my breakdown and was sorry for all the stress I must have caused. As I've previously mentioned, my dad was always a man of few words but he said he had never been prouder of me and how far I had come. He told me that I didn't need to worry when the time came and he was no longer here as he knew I would get through it as I was stronger than I gave myself credit for. This was so comforting to hear as I hadn't even shared my worries with my dad, why would I when he was going through all this. He was my dad though and knew me inside out and will have known what was going on in that head of mine. That's the kind of person he was, selfless to the end and always thinking of his family. I could write a lot more about this stage in my life and what it was like to watch your dad die in front of you but this isn't what this book's about. I just wanted to highlight the fact that this sudden loss of my dad was traumatic and devastating but it didn't break me like I thought it would. It made me realise that my breakdown, all those years ago, was an isolated incident and I think going through this was the first time that I truly believed that. If anything was going to send me back there then it would have been the loss of my dad but it didn't.

CHAPTER THIRTY-SIX

I was traumatised for some time after his death but not once did I contemplate going to the doctors and getting medication to help me get through it. I did it my way, again through counselling and speaking to someone and by just looking after myself and not pushing myself to get over things in a certain time. Grief is different for everyone and no time limit should be set on when you should be better or back at work. Everyone deals with it differently and therefore everyone should be dealt with differently. I couldn't let myself get caught up in all the sadness as I was too afraid of not getting back out of it. My dad had told me that I would be ok and I was. I made sure I carried on with my counselling for some time and even referred myself onto a residential course at one of the police convalescent homes. I was okay but I wanted to make sure I stayed that way and did everything in my power to help myself.

Not long after the death of my dad my first long term relationship since being well ended abruptly. Although this was not long after losing my dad and a similar pattern of the two losses I was subjected to prior to my breakdown, again I was okay. I think I had learnt how to acknowledge loss and also accept it and had developed a lot of these tools through counselling and past experience. Plus, again, no medication to poison that brain of mine and send me into a frenzy.

So here I was back living alone again, in a different house but grateful that my brain was still intact after the whirlwind of the past few months. I could easily have gone the other way but I didn't. Don't get me wrong I still had dark times but I managed to get through them, even my second panic attack, which again happened whilst at work.

I was on late shift responding to the numerous calls that were coming over the radio and the next minute a request was made for someone to attend a residential dwelling where there were reports of a male having been stabbed. As much as I didn't want to take that call, I did, I had to. It had been years since I attended the stabbing of the young male and I couldn't avoid these jobs any longer. I drove to the address on auto pilot, flashbacks of that incident fourteen years earlier swirling around in my head. It was so long ago but now it felt like yesterday. I happened to be first on scene again with my supervisor arriving shortly after. As I walked in the house, I was immediately faced with an absolute blood bath. A male was lying on his back drenched in blood and I soon noticed a knife on the floor and a deep wound to his thigh which I suspected had cut through one of his main arteries given the amount of blood he was swimming in. I froze for a while as I didn't think I could handle someone dying on me again but my supervisor soon snapped me out of my trance and we both began CPR until the ambulance arrived and paramedics took over. It was slightly different this time, the male was a bit older which doesn't make it better but losing a young person is always harder. He was also unconscious so I didn't need to worry about him pleading with me to save him like the last time. I moved to the side to allow paramedics to carry on with the treatment. I remember looking down at my hands and arms and they were covered in blood, as were my boots and every bit of my uniform. I was completely drenched in this man's blood. The way it felt on my skin, all wet and sticky, sent me back fourteen years to sitting in that room with that young boy whilst he had his head wrapped in a plastic bag. That was the moment then that I realised I was covered in his blood too. I said it earlier in my book, smells, touch and other significant things can send you back to a traumatic place and time in your life in an instant. I was starting to get that fuzzy feeling in my head and my heart rate was on the rise but I knew I had to hold it together just that little bit longer as I had now been instructed to get in the back of the ambulance and assist with CPR on route to hospital. I knew this male had gone but time and effort were spent trying to bring him back round. I carried out CPR all the way to hospital which was probably a ten- minute journey.

Ten minutes doesn't sound like a long time but trust me it is when you're constantly pounding on someone's chest that hard that you can hear and feel their ribs cracking under the pressure of your palms. As we got to hospital and into the resus room doctors took over and carried on but not for long as I think it had become apparent very quickly that this man was gone and every bit of his blood had left his body, a lot of which had transferred onto mine. There I was stood in another resus room, drenched in blood next to a deceased male having been stabbed. A doctor asked if I was okay and all I could do was nod. I couldn't get my words out as I knew that my panic attack was on its way and was coming fast. I needed to get out of there and quickly as I didn't want anyone to witness what was about to happen. I knew where the toilets were, and here I was again sat on the cubicle floor, heart attempting to climb out of my chest, dripping in sweat and unable to catch my breath. Memories of the last hour and the job fourteen years ago cluttering my brain. Please let it stop I thought. Why now after all this time has that job suddenly reared its head and made this situation ten times worse. My counsellor explained to me, when she diagnosed me with PTSD, that even if things aren't on your mind constantly and you think they have gone they haven't. Trauma lies dormant in your head and can explode at any time and be recalled when reminded of the slightest thing. In this case this wasn't the slightest thing, it was very similar job. Different in many ways but similar in that I was drenched in some one's blood and witnessed another horrific death.

Even though I had just experienced my second panic attack I didn't feel the need to go and see my counsellor like I did the first time, mainly due to the fact that I knew what it was and not that I was having some kind of heart attack and dying. I also knew how to calm myself down quicker through the techniques my counsellor had given me and the research I had done on panic attacks since. I knew I couldn't start to avoid certain situations because of the fear they'll trigger another attack and that is why I knew I had to shout up for this job even though I ran the risk of doing that. Something my counsellor said to me which has always stuck in my head, 'Avoiding situations can create a cycle of living in fear of fear' and that is something that I didn't want to do.

CHAPTER THIRTY-SEVEN

The nightmares and flash backs never fully went and still haven't today. I guess you always carry that pain around but eventually learn to live with it rather than let it control you. I've since discovered that the hospital I was in, shut down a number of years ago. Not for any other reason than to be sold off to property developers. I've often wanted to delve in to things more, such as why did it close, did other people suffer and get abused like I did and write about it. I've scanned the internet briefly and there are the odd bad comments, on various sites, about the place but nothing specific. I've also thought about whether to make an official complaint to the police about the things that happened to me in there. I've toyed with this idea for some time now but have come to the conclusion to let sleeping dogs lie. The main reason being that I really don't think anyone will believe me, even still to this day. Let's be honest, my medical notes, should I ever be able to retrieve them, will not be a true reflection of what happened, why would they. They wouldn't have written 'gave her no chance to respond to request of taking medication so pinned her to the floor and jabbed her knocking her out' or 'dragged the female down the corridor by her feet laughing with my colleagues and calling her names whilst she screamed and cried' I don't believe any of my notes will contain information like this at all. It would probably read something like 'We asked the female to take her medication politely and gave her ample opportunity to do this before she became aggressive with staff and had to be restrained and injected with a sedative to calm her down'. I think that would be a more accurate account of what would have been documented, even if it was complete and utter lies. I have since sent off for my notes as I'm interested to see what's in them. I've been told it may take a while and that they may not even be retrievable anymore. We shall see!

CHAPTER THIRTY-EIGHT

I'm going to skip forward now to the year 2015 when I finally met my soul mate and the person, I knew I would spend the rest of my life with, and have in fact since married this year. I know I said earlier that I told myself not to be as honest with people with fear of them using stuff against me, well I told her everything very early on and have not regretted that decision ever as she has not once thrown anything back in my face. I had finally found someone that understood mental health and showed some compassion about what I had been through. My life was finally back how I wanted it to be and in 2019 I gave birth to our beautiful daughter.

Getting pregnant always seemed like a distance dream to me even before my breakdown and even more so after it. I always thought that there would be no chance of me getting pregnant. There were a few reasons for this the main one being that I genuinely believed that the medication I was once on would have messed my body up and I wouldn't be able to conceive. Probably an irrational thought but I believed it. It also worried me that once I'd had the baby, I may suffer from post-natal depression given my previous mental health. This worry was enhanced as during my pregnancy and my meetings with my midwife, I was asked on the usual tick list whether I had ever suffered from depression or mental health related illnesses. My midwife was also a friend of ours and had no idea about my past so I was in that predicament of whether to just tick NO to all the above or be honest. Being honest was hard as one, I had to tell someone and go through my past when I had tried so hard to forget it and two, I was now worried that I would be treated differently. I decided to be honest though, as I trusted her. I had waited so long for this moment and just wanted to be treated like any other pregnant woman. For the first time in a long time, I felt different again and I really didn't like it. I understand that everyone has to be treated the same when they tick these boxes but I think people should be treated individually. For example, yes, I had had issues in the past, but I'd had not suffered from anything for a long time. I understand I may have to be referred for a quick follow up and check everything is okay, I get that. However, I didn't see the need to be referred to the perinatal mental health team for the majority of my pregnancy, especially when I was well again and had been for so long. It only highlights things again and starts that paranoia that something may go wrong.

I never told my mum about this as I saw no reason, plus I didn't want her to start worrying about anything.

However, this was taken out of my hands as they rang my mum at her house asking for me and introduced themselves as the Perinatal Mental Health Team. Obviously, my mum automatically panicked thinking there was something wrong and that I hadn't kept her in the loop. To get something minor wrong like a phone number was such a huge mistake and had such an impact on me as, again, all those memories from years ago came flooding back about how inadequate these services were and I started to feel abnormal again, and like I was being watched for no reason. That said I made a complaint and they couldn't have been more apologetic but the damage was done now. I really can't understand why they would have my mums home phone number on record when I have not lived there for over fifteen years. Luckily, I had an amazing pregnancy and did not suffer any form of depression afterwards.

I have, however, since been diagnosed with epilepsy which has taken a long time to diagnose. It was incredibly frustrating to have been examined by so many neurologists only to leave each time with no answers. I felt like no one was taking me seriously or listening to me about my symptoms. I found it hard to trust health professionals again, of any sort, since everything that went on and I believed at the time that people didn't believe me due to my past mental health issues. I have had symptoms for a long time and a lot of the investigations and tests that I have had carried out could not pin point why I was having my seizures. At first my consultant suggested that I could be suffering from psychogenic non epileptic seizures (PNES) due to the traumatic time I endured through my psychotic breakdown. I had never heard of these but have since been told that the seizures and symptoms are the same as epilepsy but that the dissociate seizures are not caused by abnormal electrical activity in the brain. Instead, it's thought they are a physical reaction to distressing triggers such as sensations, thoughts, emotions and difficult situations. Some experts say dissociate seizures are the brain's way of 'shutting down' to protect itself from overwhelming distress. About one in five people referred to hospital for seizures are diagnosed with dissociative seizures.

Although my consultant has diagnosed me with epilepsy rather than nonepileptic seizures, he stated that it could still be a consideration as to why I suffer from the seizures and contribute to it in some way. Some people have both dissociative and epileptic seizures and I could still fall into this bracket which my consultant has advised will be explored more in the future. I was eventually prescribed epilepsy medication as my consultant was content that my symptoms were consistent with epilepsy. I was scared about taking the medication at first after reading the side effects but did it gradually and the correct way and have been okay. The brain is a powerful organ and although it has not been one hundred per cent confirmed yet that I could have both there is a strong possibility after the trauma I went through, especially whilst in hospital, and the fact it gradually got worse over the years.

CHAPTER THIRTY-NINE

There are many things that helped me survive my 'Episode' and too many to probably list but I will sum up what got me through the worst years of my life, the first one, and most important one, being the help and support from my family and friends. I wouldn't have got through this without them. As already mentioned, the majority of my friends I am still in touch with today. However, the odd friend I am not and totally understand why they felt the need to distance themselves from me. If they are reading this book today and they will know who they are, I just want to say thank you for everything you did for me.

Anticipating what could happen and have a plan was vital to me. If I felt I was relapsing or worrying about something I would talk to a counsellor about possible major stressors and things I needed to watch for, and made sure that my counsellor was someone that I felt I could trust. I always tried to identify things that I could do to avoid a crisis and still do that to this day. 'Keeping Hope' was key to me and I always reminded myself that I was not an illness and that I had just been ill. I tried not to accept negative assumptions about labels and tried to see that what I went through was a 'blip' in my life. I gave myself time to recover, years of it in fact and I eventually learnt how to give myself credit for what I was able to do and how far I had come. I was responsible for my life, no one else. Yes, family and friends can offer advice and be there for you but no one else could do it for me and that is why I knew I had to find the strength to keep going.

You have to remember that psychosis is a no-fault illness and no matter what answers you search for no one is to blame. It brings many losses which in my case was the loss of my relationship and my career for a short period of time. Looking back on it now, I went through a grief process to heal from the loss of that relationship. During that grief process I went through a lot of anger at myself for messing things up and hurting people, but most of all anger at the system and those that didn't listen to me and instead put me in that psych unit and tortured me more. I still carry that anger around with me to this day but not as often as it was. I did a lot of bargaining with myself throughout my recovery, thinking if I do this, things will be back to the way they were. If I just take my medication, If I just pray (which I'm not even a religious person), if I just work hard enough. The truth is, psychosis changes people's lives but with successful adaptation, the changes can be positive.

Educating myself was definitely a major part of my recovery and moving forward. At the beginning I struggled more as I didn't know what was happening to me or couldn't give myself a label so literally felt like I had lost my mind and would never get it back. When I was discharged from hospital and took my recovery seriously, I started to educate myself about the things that affected me which included my specific medical condition/diagnosis. This also included learning specific techniques from my counsellor such as breathing exercise and thinking processes. This helped with panic attacks as well. Each day I would set myself goals but take it one step at a time. I set small, specific short-term goals for myself and then tried to stay focussed on them.

Pat Risser, a long-term mental health advocate, uses the analogy of a ladder. You have been going through life for a long time, going from one rung to the other. When you experience psychosis, it's like falling off the ladder. It takes some time to recover, and when you start to feel better again you have a tendency to want to jump right back to where you are. I was advised by my counsellor at the time that if I did that, there was a good chance I would crash. I found that if I was to succeed, I had to take it slowly, one step at a time which worked as I eventually found my way back and even beyond that as I found new skills and experiences which have been helpful to me going forward.

Everyone is vulnerable to psychosis, but some develop it more easily than others. Having come to the conclusion that mine was drug induced (prescribed), I no longer feel vulnerable or have the worry of a relapse or reoccurrence in the future but there is no harm in educating yourself on triggers which is what I have done. I always make sure I get as much sleep as I can as lack of sleep can have all different effects on your mental health. I try to reduce my stress levels as best I can and do this through exercise. Anniversaries of traumatic deaths and in my case my dads can be a trigger but I always turn it into a happy time and remember the good about him rather than dwelling on the last hour of his life whilst he was dying. The main thing I always make sure is that I never take any medication, even if I'm prescribed it, without reading the side effects beforehand. To be honest I very rarely take it unless I absolutely have to and that is only the odd prescription of anti-biotics or over the counter paracetamol. I always try to steer clear of any medication.

CHAPTER FORTY

Being sectioned was a really horrendous experience. But, at the same time, I survived it. I have debated long and hard as to whether to write this book and in the beginning only wrote it from a therapeutic point. I have completely bared my soul and even my family will read stuff that I have never spoken to them about. I was worried that people who aren't aware of what happened to me will now think differently of me having now read my book. However, these thoughts were outweighed by the fact that I finally feel content in my life and what I went through and I am no longer ashamed of an illness that I did not choose to get. It has made me stronger than ever and taken me along the path that I ended up on and found my happily ever after. If sharing my experience can help one person through their own battle with mental health then it was worth every second of my time writing this book. It may not seem it at the time but there is light at the end of the tunnel, you've just got to be prepared to keep digging!

My acceptance has enabled me to feel proud and grateful for getting through it and to where I am today, both personally and professionally. I count myself lucky as not everyone does recover. All my hard work and determination enabled me to pick up my police career after my debilitating period of mental illness but I'm aware isn't the case for everyone, and that stigma is still very much alive and kicking. I can honestly say that it's only in the last few years that I can talk about my experience without feeling ashamed or labelled.

Although I'm fully recovered and leading a normal life again, I still suffer from the odd bout of 'health anxiety' from time to time. I don't think that will ever go. I go through stages with this and can be okay for a long time but when I'm ever stressed about anything it can rear its head again. It's only minor in comparison but feels huge to me at the time. I have learnt more and more over the years to control this and rationalise things in my head before rushing off to the doctors to get things checked. I can't and won't let things like this consume me anymore. My psychosis revolved around this fear of dying as I was never like that before I became ill and will never fully understand why I fixated on this during my illness. However, I have come to accept that having health anxiety from time to time is a small price to pay after what I went through and ultimately, I survived it.

I have since retired from the police force following an assault on duty resulting in an injury which unfortunately couldn't be fixed. I was devastated to have to leave but prior to going I had clawed my way back to the Public

Protection Unit, the unit I was once told I would never go back on. I proved them wrong, and showed myself that I did have the strength and determination to do whatever I wanted and that involved getting my dream job back, and even if it was only for a short time, I did it! I genuinely believe that if you want something bad enough and fight hard enough for it then it is achievable. You've just got to want it enough and not give up. Since retiring I have continued my passion for helping vulnerable people with both mental health problems and other personal issues. I'm a great believer in fate and although I've lost the job, I had wanted to do from the age of five, I have still gone on to help people in a different way. It has also given me the time to write this book and finally tell my story, which has not only been therapeutic to me but also highlighted once more how precious life really is and that life is for living.

Recovery is finding what works for you, no matter how large or how small that step. Believing that recovery is possible is so important, whatever that path looks like for you. Just as recovery can mean different things for different people, so can hope. These days I find hope in the everyday. My cup of tea in the morning, my cuddles with my two girls, to the pitter patter of my fingers on the keyboard writing this story.

The advice I'd have for someone newly diagnosed or feeling very lost and out of control is it gets better. It might seem hopeless but managing your condition is possible and with the right help and support, you can still go on to live a fulfilling life. My dark days made me stronger, or maybe I already was strong and they made me prove it. Always remember tough times never last but tough people do.

The End

ACKNOWLEDGEMENTS

There are so many people I'd like to thank but too many to personally mention. First and foremost, I'd like to thank my mum and dad for all their support during that horrendous time and for fighting to get me out of there and ultimately saving me. My sister for dropping everything and coming home to be with me and always having my back.

I'm deeply grateful to each and every one of my friends past and present for standing by me and always being there for me no matter how hard things got. Also, to Lisa, Bex, Leah and Louise for taking on the role of proof readers and not forgetting my new found friend Melanie for her excellent ideas and support. An extra special thank you to one of my friends who I am no longer in contact with now but was there no matter what and supported me in ways I can never repay. He will know who he is.

Thank you to my counsellor Zoe for giving me the push I needed to write this book and inspiring me and to

Acknowledgements

Publishing Push for all their hard work and commitment with publishing my story.

Last but not least thank you to my wife Leanne and our two beautiful girls for all their support whilst writing this. I couldn't have done this without you.

Milton Keynes UK
Ingram Content Group UK Ltd.
UKHW020003080724
445035UK00002B/19